The Complete Guide for the Romantically Challenged Male

The Complete Guide for the Romantically Challenged Male

John P. Borden

Writers Club Press
New York Lincoln Shanghai

The Complete Guide for the Romantically Challenged Male

Writers Club Press
an imprint of iUniverse, Inc.

For information address:
iUniverse, Inc.
2021 Pine Lake Road, Suite 100
Lincoln, NE 68512
www.iuniverse.com

ISBN: 0-595-25610-4 (pbk)
ISBN: 0-595-65210-7 (cloth)

Printed in the United States of America

"In this common-place world everyone is said to be a romantic who either admires a fine thing or does one."

—Alexander Pope

This book is for

MEN ONLY

Women caught reading this book will be punished............possibly.

To Peg

My wife, best friend, soul mate and primary reason I am a romantic.

Contents

Preface xiii

Part I   *WHY*

CHAPTER 1   Romantic...To Be or Not to Be...And Why. 3

Part II   *WHO*

CHAPTER 2   Foundation Relationship. 13

Part III   *HOW*

CHAPTER 3   Where to Begin 21

CHAPTER 4   Remembering...and/or Not Forgetting. 25

CHAPTER 5   Hint Gathering 29

Part IV   *WHAT*

CHAPTER 6   The Little Things 35

CHAPTER 7   Flowers 41

CHAPTER 8   Words. 47

CHAPTER 9   Chivalry 61

CHAPTER 10   Gifts and Presents 67

CHAPTER 11   Touching 77

Part V   WHEN AND WHERE

CHAPTER 12   Occasions 83

CHAPTER 13   Going Out and Staying In 89

Part VI   OTHER STUFF

CHAPTER 14   Cautions 97

CHAPTER 15   Hard Cases 103

CHAPTER 16   Sex 107

CHAPTER 17   Curable or Not 111

CHAPTER 18   Technology 113

CHAPTER 19   Advanced Topics 117

Part VII ONE FOR THE GIPPER

CHAPTER 20   Give It a Try 125

Part VIII SUMMARY OF GUIDES AND LISTS

SUMMARY 129

CONCLUSION 151

Preface

This book is a guide for men in the art and science of romantic gestures. It is intended for any man who has any feelings whatsoever. If feelings are present, then some are probably toward another human being and of a romantic nature. While men have romantic feelings, they receive poor marks in sharing or expressing these feelings. In this book are numerous hints, suggestions, dos and don'ts. They are intended to help the reader improve his comfort and effectiveness in translating romantic feelings into gestures and developing comfort in conveying or delivering these gestures.

Humor is used throughout because that's the way I think and because it will, hopefully, make the book more readable for men. Some men have a real discomfort in this whole realm of romantic ideas, thoughts and expressions. Possibly, a bit of humor will ease the pain.

In the beginning…or reasonably close to it, you and your wife, lover or girlfriend were hopelessly in romantic love. Most relationships begin by being in romantic love. A few still are. A few more are in the pits with little hope for rescue. But most of us remain in love, but with a love that may not still be called romantic love.

This is not to say that anything is wrong. Love changes over time. It may be more romantic or less. For some, the romantic part isn't there or it has taken a back seat, or just lacks the emphasis it once had.

It is for those in the majority middle ground that this book was written. This is a guide to romantic actions for men. It is intended for men who want to get a fresh idea or two all the way to the hard case man who doesn't have a clue of what romance is, why it is appropriate and why it involves him.

Most of the books on romance tend to be by women for women. This observation can be confirmed by looking at the magazines and other stuff at the end of the checkout aisle in the grocery store. There are a few books for men but most of them are by women or by an MD or PHD type. This book is different in that it is just one man conversing with another saying: "Hey it's OK to be romantic." Here is what works and enjoy reading about it.

Maybe this is a good point to address the topic of sexism. You will note that occasionally I cast men and women in stereotypical roles. If readers get hyper over that, I would suggest that they stop reading immediately and get a book on enjoying humor. The author of this epistle (that's me) enjoys humor. Also, the author, some say, has the greatest regard for women and is not a sexist in any form. However, it must be absolutely clear that there are differences between men and women. I'm sure everyone can grant that.

While we are on the sexist topic, it may be appropriate to discuss terms. I intend to use the terms women and men, ladies and gentlemen, wife and husband, partner, lover, friend, sweetheart and more. I hope no one gets upset. I understand that some terms get some folks on edge. If you want to get upset I suppose you will. My apologies if you don't like the phrase or term. The point I am trying to express is that there are many terms for your relationship with another person. For some out there one set of words is fine. For another, they won't be. Also, relationships vary tremendously and not all will be found under the marriage umbrella. Just be open and look at the thoughts. Thanks.

Organization of the book follows the who, what, where, why, and when and how pattern. Why is first with Chapter I, "To be or not to be romantic…and why". Chapter two starts Who with "Foundation/Relationship". Chapter three, "Where to Begin," is the beginning of the How chapters with Chapter four "Remembering and/or Not Forgetting," Chapter five, "Hint Gathering,"….

"…John…I don't understand, why are you listing the chapters here when there is a perfectly good index spelled out on the next page?"

In case you're wondering, that statement was from a reader, actually a reader critic. Their statements appear here and throughout the text.

This one is right. No need to repeat the index. The chapters of this guide will treat varieties of expressions and some do's and don'ts. While it is intended that you read all the way through, please feel free to jump around.

Enjoy and good expressing. Best of everything to you as you embark on your romantic journey.

PART I
WHY

1

Romantic...To Be or Not to Be...And Why

"In the meanest hut is a romance, if you but knew the heart's there."

—*Varnhagen Von Ense*

This book is about being romantic. What is being romantic? A working definition is simply "doing those things" which express romance. Of course, that answer begs another question: What is romance? Romance is just a kind of love. So that being romantic is no more than doing loving things. The hard part is not the definition but the "things." The hard part is what, when, where, why and occasionally who.

But wait, we need a bit of a side trip. Things are changing. Relationships are changing. Rules are changing. Roles are changing. It used to be that we would picture a guy in St. Louis who just read the last paragraph to his buddies and is yukking away at the terms love and romance. We need to stop this right now. "Hey Bud, or whatever your name is. Yeh, you in St. Louis. Why the yukking? Oh you thought that men talking about love and romance was sissy stuff? Well let me tell you a few things.... First, you would not even be here if your parents didn't experience a bit of love and romance. Second, you say you are a church person, then look at the Bible, it's full of the idea of love; you are even commanded to love. And finally, you want me to tell Mrs.

3

Bud you were yukking over the terms love and romance? That's better."

Sorry about that. You know it is really curious what some consider as being manly or macho. Some get so much into the outward appearances, signs and symbols that they forget that we are first and foremost human beings, persons. Human beings or persons are social animals. As a matter of fact, persons need to relate to one another or they die. (References to studies not supplied since this is not a scholarly work, nor is it for a grade.) As persons relate with each other, love will occur. To deny this is inhuman. To make fun of it is a sign of immaturity. To make fun of love and expressing feelings is a behavior that we went through when we thought that bodily sounds were the funniest thing going. And this was a very early age. At least it was for most of us.

In this book, the stature of a man is partly measured by his ability to have and share feelings. This is manliness. In fact not to have feelings and not to share those feelings may indicate some real problems. And everyone knows that real men don't have real problems. That is definitely not macho.

I think I just dug my first hole. Try this. If it is manly to have and share feelings, why is it that we seem to have difficulty in doing so or catch the rap that we men are never romantic or romantic enough? Having posed the question I will now sidestep it. The answer to the question is unconditionally complicated and beyond the scope of this book. (How was that?) More to the point is that most men feel more romantic than their actions demonstrate. Ah Ha! If the feelings are there why don't they come forth in actions? Here we can observe that either we have been discouraged from showing these feelings or we just don't know how.

Our view of men and romance used to be the St. Louis model. But now we see more and more men listening to Dr. Laura and being open to feelings and this whole topic.

There is a risk of getting deeply into the psychology and sociology of feelings expression, male and female roles, needs and so forth. Again, let others treat that. This guide is a roadmap of how to demonstrate those feelings not why they are there or whether we express them adequately. Is there a need for a guide? The answer seems to be yes, based on a ton of input. Most of the input comes from my precious wife. I tend to do the romantic things for her. She appreciates them. She does romantic things for me. Our lives and marriage are richer. Others note some of the things and say, "That's so great or that's so sweet or I wish Bud would do that…" and on it goes. Bud, you still with me? Great! The thought then came to write a book. I asked a number of women what they thought and the general reaction was that they would be the first in line to get a copy.

<u>Why Bother</u>

We need to have a working assumption that there is someone you love or would like to love and that you have a strong enough feeling to want to show that love. While the orientation is to marriage and to man and woman, the reader can apply the guide to any variation applicable. Of course, that can go to extremes. The gesture of a hunter giving his Golden Retriever a rose on the anniversary of the dog's first pheasant is probably lost on the dog.

Back to romantic love. If we enjoy the blessing of romantic love we are bursting to share it, to demonstrate it, to celebrate it. In my case, the object of that love is my wife, Peg. We will soon be celebrating over 40 years of marriage. Peg and I have been through a lot, mostly pleasurable, but a measure of pain as well. Out of this, our love has continued to grow. Part of the reason is that we have bathed each other in expressions of love. There are two very important points to make at this juncture:

1. The sharing of expressions of love is the reason love grows and is the result of love that has grown, and

2. Most of the expressions are little things individually, but add up to a tremendous relationship.

Exploring each point merits some time. The first point is that expressions produce and nurture love as well as grow out of love. It is really quite simple. If someone does something nice for you, you want to do something nice to or for him or her. Add to that the very important notion that love does not keep score and you have an ever-growing environment of expression.

Score keeping is an interesting concept. It works in competitive environments such as sports, social status, class rank and business. It does not work in romance. IT DOES NOT WORK IN ROMANCE. Score keeping seldom spends much time or energy on ties. Instead the whole idea is to determine a winner and by process of elimination, a loser or group of losers. Romance can and should be a win-win process. Both parties win. There is no loser. If there are two winners and no losers, then score keeping is not only unnecessary, it cannot take place. In romantic matters, the whole idea is <u>wanting</u> to do something or do more than what is being done for you. Score keeping in love and romance means that you feel the <u>obligation</u> to do something. That's not going to work effectively or for long. It is also not going to work if the orientation is on winning instead of giving.

Imagine, if you will, a boy and girl sitting on a swing on a porch on a pleasant warm summer evening. They have just shared watching a magnificent sunset. He reaches in his pocket and pulls out a long jewelry box, which he presents to the girl. She opens the box and finds a very nice bracelet. She says, "It's just lovely. You shouldn't have. This isn't any occasion, why did you do this...." And so on. The score keeping response is, "You're right, I shouldn't have. Here, give it back and I will present it on a regular occasion." Another score keeping response could be, "Well, you bought me that sweater last month, so I figured it was my turn. After all, I don't want you to get ahead or anything." You may not be a rocket scientist and don't need to be to figure out that those responses are not only cool, but cold. They are actually put-downs and cruel. The words totally wipe out the impact of the gift. On the other hand, the non-score keeping responses of, "I just wanted to," or, "A special gift for a special person," or, "I really wanted to see if your smile or the sunset is more beautiful, and your smile is by far," will add to the gift and its presentation. In fact, a good response or statement upon presentation is like 1+1=3.

Oh, by the way, that last response about the smile and the sunset? That's undoubtedly a more advanced response. Don't try it if it isn't you. After all, the objective is not to shock her into cardiac arrest.

Another example of this concept comes from the saying that a successful marriage grows out of each party giving 60%. The point being that if you give more than you expect to receive, you are not scorekeeping, but just plain giving. Of course, there is always the possibility of a 99% giver. Chances are that this person does not know how to receive and needs some help. A healthy relationship has both giving and receiving. It should be balanced.

There needs to be a bit of reality checking at this point. If a relationship is bad, romantic expressions won't change that. A sound relationship will grow with the expression of love and romance. Growth assumes that there is something there which has already started and is alive.

Can the expressions be overdone? Sure. I recall a speaker I once heard who was describing something which could be over or under done. His example was holding a bird. If you hold it too tightly, you will kill it. If you hold it too loosely, it will fly away.

This gets us to the reason that this book contains guidelines—not rules. Each reader must take each thought, hint or idea and determine if it fits his situation, her situation, and their situation. We must all avoid too much, too little, or the inappropriate, even of a good thing. We don't want cardiac arrest or someone losing their dentures over an unexpected gesture from a, here-to-fore unromantic blob or slob or Bob.

The second point made above is that being romantic is a process for sharing many little expressions. This is critically important to each reader. What this is saying is that regardless of where you are—you just met, you would like to meet, or you have been married for fifty years the next gesture need only be a little thing. Whether or not another gesture follows that gesture is up to you. Whether the gestures become more frequent or more significant is also up to you. Remember the bird. Also, look to the second quote beginning Chapter Six.

What is Romantic Expression

To some, a romantic expression might be cruise tickets left on the breakfast table or a diamond ring in a glass of champagne or a delivery of 5 dozen roses, etc. Yes, these are romantic expressions but of gigantic proportions. Just picture this as a first date; you pick her up in a limo, five dozen roses in the limo, and cruise tickets over the talk at the restaurant, a diamond in the champagne. Come on. You have probably killed the bird. If you haven't killed the bird and she buys all that, what do you do next, and what does she expect from the relationship?

The essence of romantic expression is simplicity and sincerity. It is based on feeling, not financial status. It is a gentle smile. When she asks, "Why are you smiling?" It's a simple, "I'm glad I met you," or "I'm glad I married you." It's a simple flower on the car seat before a trip. It's a card from out of town when on a business trip without an occasion. It's a playful wink. It's a hug.

It is something that enters through the eyes, ears, or other senses and goes immediately to the heart where it produces a gentle but significant tug. It says, "I love you." It does not say, "I'm rich and powerful or important." The message is nurturing the recipient, not aggrandizing the sender.

Some may now think that this book is directed toward a certain class of men. Well, it is in the sense that this is a guidebook for the romantically challenged. But what else? There is no pattern of economics or intellect or education or position or any other attribute that defines the romantically challenged. Maybe the wealthy can buy lots of cars, diamonds and furs. But this can be done without a shred of romantic impact. Maybe some don't speak well in fluid, flowery terms. It isn't the language. It is the simplicity and sincerity that is used. There is nothing in this book intended to put anyone or any characteristic down. We can all improve—some more than others. Some who read this book might be advanced romantics who have already achieved their advanced rating by doing most everything herein. Well, congratulations to you, if you are one of them. You can then appreciate this book as an affirmation.

PART II
WHO

2

Foundation Relationship

o o o o o o o o o o o o o o o o o o o o o o o o o o o o o o

"When the ancients said a work well begun was half done, they meant to impress the importance of always endeavoring to make a good beginning."

—*Polybius*

Very seldom will this guide fit a situation when you have just met a person. Picture this scene in the movies. The scene is a party. The very handsome young man looks across the room and sees her. She sees him. Their eyes lock for several minutes. They walk toward each other. He takes her hand. Their eyes are still locked on each other. He swallows hard, takes a deep breath, and says, "I don't know who you are but won't you share my life forever? Destiny brought us to this room so that our spirits could make contact. Walking across the room, I have learned to cherish you. If you say no, my life is over, finished. I shall rot as a shell of my former self, all purpose for living stripped from me by your failure to satisfy my unquenchable love for you...."

You can imagine the rest of the scene. She, of course, has to say yes, and say it as eloquently. Then they stroll hand in hand toward the full moon with the credits rolling up their backs. If that is what you are looking for, try romance novels or selected movies.

Romantic feelings and actions are more normally played out in the context of an existing relationship. What that relationship is will vary. It may vary widely, but a relationship is where we start.

The phrase…"in the context of an existing relationship"…is very important. Unless there is an underlying love, desire for love, or potential for love, then romantic feelings are not there. I use love because it is the essence of romance and is what we all want to give and receive. Can the word *regard* be used? Certainly. Use any word you wish and use any degree of intensity you wish, nurturing, of course. The only important part is to realize that a relationship, a positive relationship, is the foundation for feeling romantic and wanting to act romantically.

Of course, there are exceptions. Take the situation where a separation between a man and woman occurs and divorce is being discussed. What then if he sends her flowers…. The flowers are a romantic gesture but the relationship is on the rocks. Well, maybe it is and maybe it isn't. If the message behind the flowers is, "I deep down still love you a tiny bit and want to see if there is any hope left," then maybe the flowers will be a small step and a POSITIVE step. Of course, the opposite could be true and the message behind the flowers could be, "I hate you, good-bye," and by the way the flowers will wilt soon—as our relationship has." Ugh. No question about it. These flowers are not a romantic gesture. Note that the gesture is the same.

The romantic gesture is like rain. For something to grow it must first have roots and leaves. It must have germinated and begun. With this foundation, this beginning, growth can take place. The gesture can nurture what is there. Too much can flood or wash away. Too little…and wilting will occur.

In addition to there being a relationship, it is assumed that the relationship is positive! What about the *"I'm sorry"* gesture from the dude who is deep in the doghouse? Still valid. The gesture is saying that he wants the relationship to continue, and hopefully, get past this thing that has prompted the *"I'm sorry,"* and go forward. Will it work? Ah Ha! Who knows?

Now we hear from a man in Fort Smith, Arkansas, shouting, "I got this silly book because you promised better romance!" Not true, Fort Smith. This is a guide, not a guarantee. Those who ease into a more frequent or different use of romantic gestures will probably find a better relationship, assuming one exists. But those who are insensitive to their significant other, insensitive to timing, gesture, message and context will probably fail. Some many never get it right, but a word to the wise should be sufficient. Remember the rain. Romantic gestures are intended to nurture.

Treating Your Love as a Friend

On one wall in our living room we have a number of wall hangings. One is a saying, "Happiness is being married to your best friend." My wife treasures this. It does reflect how we try to live. It is also an expression where nurture is very much a part of the process.

I hear a reader-critic asking why? "Why do you want your lover as a friend?" OK, that's a fair question. Take the stylized image of newlyweds as constantly running to the bedroom where they do it again and again in some frenzied fashion similar to the driving force found in salmon on their way to spawn. That's nice, but usually not the case. A friend from Macon, Georgia, now comments, "Well, we do it every night, three times, and have for the last forty years." Well, that is indeed commendable but does not qualify for some kind of award or monument…well maybe it does. But most, a very significant most, experience some less frequent or intense pattern of sexual expression. More on that later. The point is that you are with a very neat person, you are not in bed, you are fully clothed, the chores are done, and it's not an occasion for you to be out with the boys or for her to be out with the girls. So what do you do? You go somewhere, you talk, and you share life. It's a lot more fun if you are doing it with a friend.

So, where does this go? If your partner is not a friend, work on it. If your partner is a friend, work on it. The point being, work on it.

Phrases for Friends

• Let's just stay here tonight.

- Let's just go out tonight.

- How about a walk?

- How was your day?

- What would you like to do that we haven't done?

- Can I help you with something?

- Are you as happy as you could be...?

- What can I do to make your life more enjoyable?

- I enjoy spending time with you.

- You look sad. Anything I can do?

Friends spend time together. Look at your use of time and your partner's use of time. Is it balanced? Are you all work and no play? Is your play strictly a *guy* thing? Is she always with the girls? You and your partner need to be balanced. If friendship is part of your program, is sufficient time being allocated to cultivating the friendship? In other words, take stock. Do an inventory.

After doing your inventory, act upon it. If you are really cultivating the friendship, sit down with your partner and discuss the balance. If it is awkward for you, then ease into it with some small items such as the phrases above.

There is no question about relationships changing over time. They do. Some become stronger, some become weaker. Usually, the determining factor is how much work is put into the relationship. Going back to our garden example.... In addition to needing the rain of romantic gestures, the garden also needs cultivating, weeding, and other forms of nurture to work.

It is very sad to see some relationships approach major changes such as the empty nest, poor health or retirement, and not be prepared. It is very possible to get caught up in the daily routines and suddenly discover that little or no substance for an ongoing relationship has been built. An example is a wife saying to her husband after he retires, "I married you for life, but not for lunch everyday."

If the partners are not used to spending time together, enjoying each other's retirement can be deadly. I use deadly because retirement resulting in inactivity has been shown to contribute to early death. Similarly, kids leaving the house can leave a large hole in the activity level and also the feelings area. The other area of major change is health, where surprises can alter our life significantly.

The guy with a stroke whose life was golf needs a friend. The woman who lost a breast to cancer needs a friend. The best friend is, hopefully, the one with whom you have spent much of your life. But to be a friend at the time of need means that the friendship has been building for some time.

"Wait, author person," comes the outcry from the tens of thousands of golfers, hunters, card players, and of course, the fishermen, who say, "How dare this author person attack these sacred activities, which are men's rights and privileges." To which author person responds, Whoa!! I have not called for drastic change. I have suggested more balance. If this rankles you, it may be an indication that balance is truly in need of being examined.

There is no question about the need for men to do men things and women to do women things. But where a man and a woman enter into a relationship, the relationship requires we do things together as well as doing men and women things. Balance. Balance. Balance.

Mothers as Girlfriends

In your romantic planning, remember that your mother is also one of your girlfriends, or should be. If you relate well with your mother, consider taking her on a date or consider any of the appropriate gestures mentioned. Your mother will appreciate the attention greatly.

Hopefully, your special person will honor your relationship with your mother and not only allow you the time for some special attention but encourage it. After all, she may also be a mother and will appreciate her children seeing a good role model in action. It is also said that if any woman wants to see how she will be treated, she should look at how her man treats his mother.

It is generally true that the stronger the love is between two people, the more love becomes available to share with others. A strong love between a man and woman will usually involve loving feelings toward both families and particularly the mothers involved.

Now that we have covered this why and who, it is time for how.

PART III
HOW

3

Where to Begin

"Let us watch well our beginnings, and the results will manage themselves."

—*Alexander Clark*

The key to using romantic gestures is to use the KISS concept, or KEEP IT SIMPLE, STUDENT (I know, it originally was stupid, but I just can't call you stupid.) Throughout the guide, there are reality checks or cautions. The reason for this caution is based on our human nature causing us to occasionally use what we know in the wrong situation, at the wrong time or overly much. Remember our story of the diamond on the first date. You don't use a howitzer to hunt flies, or you don't very often. More on that under the chapter entitled, "Cautions." Let us return to the concept of simplicity.

The first part of simplicity is to not do anything more than what is natural and befitting. You may then ask, "What is natural and befitting?" The answer begins by being realistic about you and your relationship.

Suppose that you are one of those who believe that Saturdays are for golf events as sanctioned by God and not to be interfered with in any way. A flower on the kitchen table with a simple note saying, "Thank you for letting Saturdays be golf," is a great gesture. Or just, "Thank you." How about, "Let's do something special together when I return."

Another situation could be the suds sucking super sports stud or SSSSS or S^5, which is S to the fifth power. This is the male who is glued to the TV during certain regularly scheduled high religious events. He could quietly say, "Thank you," or "Thank you for putting up with this." If this same SSSSS turned off the TV, went into the kitchen and said, "My precious, most treasured flower, may I have the honor of reading to you some selected poems…" he is likely to have his wife calling 911. Regardless of what kind of a lady she is, there are gestures that are appropriate and others that are inappropriate. What is offered is a shopping list of suggestions and hints. You need to be selective.

The nature of your relationship, as well as the nature of the occasion and the situation is also important. Taking the daughter of the minister a gift from Victoria's Secret on your first date to be opened in front of her parents is not a good move. The comfort zone of the gesture needs to reflect the relationship, situation, and occasion with all being taken into account. There is more on comfort zone a bit later.

After considering the relationship between you and yours, consider the message of the gesture. An example is the confusion between sex and romance. Sex can be romantic. Certainly passion is part of love. But sometimes sex is routine, obligatory or even selfish. None of those terms is romantic. The important observation is that the truly romantic gesture is saying nothing of direct benefit for the giver of the gesture. Instead, it is saying, I love you, I appreciate you, you are special to me, and I cherish you. These are expressions of nurture, of giving, not getting. A key criterion is whether the gesture is nurturing.

Beginning is very relative. To most, this guide will enforce what they are already doing. It might give some new ideas and may serve as a prod to do a bit more. To some, beginning is an accurate and terrifying word. Those are the ones whose significant other said, "He hasn't got a single romantic bone in his body." If you are one of those, where do you start?

The longest journey begins with a single step and thus a first step must be sought. Study all of the gestures in this book and pick the one or several that say what *you feel* and are safest for you. The most important part of beginning is not to be discouraged or defeated. Don't reach for the moon and try a grandiose gesture. Don't do something non-nurturing. For example, if your significant other is overweight, forget candy. It sends the wrong message. If she is allergic to a lot of things, be careful with flowers, wool and so on.

What if the gesture goes unnoticed or unappreciated? That's OK. You have succeeded in being safe, but more important is that you have done a romantic thing. A thing once done is easier to do the next time. Try again or try something a bit different.

What if all seems to fail? In that case, talk to your love. "I would like to be more romantic, but I don't know where to start or what you want." Actually, that is one heck of a romantic gesture all by itself.

Are there truly unromantic persons incapable of giving or receiving romantic gestures, even the smallest? I suppose so but would guess that they are really rare and probably have other books they and their significant other should be reading instead of this one.

So now, you have begun. You have tried a few gestures or added a few to your existing style. Feel good? Giving always feels good. Did you get something back? Chances are you did. Most gestures will get a "Thank you," "How sweet," or "That was nice of you." Remember, you are not doing this to get something, but it sure feels good when you do. That's the great part of this whole thing. Being romantic is giving. Giving blesses the giver and the receiver. Congratulations.

Beginners Questions

- Am I sensitive to our relationship?

- Does the gesture fit the situation?

- Is the gesture nurturing?

- Is this a simple step?

- Was I sincere in my feelings?

- How was it received?

- What is next?

- Did she like that I did something but not like that particular thing?

- Was it the right or wrong time?

- Did I feel good?

4

Remembering…and/or Not Forgetting

o o o o o o o o o o o o o o o o o o o o o o o o o o o o o o
"The World does not need so much to be informed as reminded."

—*Hannah More*

Remembering is often linked with memory. "That's poppycock," states a reader from East Moline, Illinois. "I have a great memory but always get into trouble by not knowing what I should remember," he continues. Then adds, "I'm constantly getting this 'why didn't you know this or think that or realize the other'." Well, yea for you East Moline. You have unlocked the beginning of this chapter. The beginning observation is to be sensitive to what is to be remembered.

Sensitivity

Probably the most obvious is sensitivity to dates; birthday, Mother's Day, Valentines Day, and of course, the one that gets the most males into the most trouble—THE ANNIVERSARY. What may not be obvious is that anniversaries come in many forms. Most relate the word anniversary with the wedding date. Frequently, the greatest penalty comes from forgetting the marriage anniversary. Some also wish to celebrate or remember the anniversary of starting a job, the first kiss, the first…. Don't stop at anniversaries. Other dates can include parents and kids birthdays, the regular dates for a bridge club or nights out with the girls.

So what else beyond dates? How about hints about gifts or events or occasions, or nice things to do or what she likes to do, and on and on.

The key is not the list of items to be sensitive to. This whole book is a list of things to be sensitive to. The key is to be sensitive. When a man moves from listing obligations to the position of trying to practice "what can I do that will be romantic," then sensitivity begins to be natural. So we begin with the obligations of key dates and move into sensitivity that is a natural part of wanting to show love. If the sensitivity is there, the next step is to pick up signals. But I am getting ahead of myself. There is an entire chapter on hints. In fact, it is the very next chapter. If you are sensitive, you will pick up signals or hints.

Help

Some folks are naturals. They just have this gift or talent for always remembering whatever is to be remembered. It must be nice. I'm sure not in that group. Most of us need some help.

The most common kind of do-it-yourself help is a planning calendar. This can be self-drawn on a piece of paper, a day, week, month or year planner, or a computer program. Whatever it is, it has space to note things to be remembered by date. It is a simple task to keep an extra sheet of paper, which has on it those things that recur. Her birthday and anniversary are always on the same date. Each year when you get your new calendar from the bank, or whatever, sit down and log in your critical dates. If you want to really do it well, put in entries a week or so ahead of the major occasion and say, Birthday in one week, buy and plan NOW." This kind of help is easy and simple.

If a calendar is difficult, consider enlisting the help of another. This can be a secretary, if you have that kind of a position, or an associate or any friend. Some folks enjoy being organized and keeping track of everything. You are bound to know one or two. Request a favor, cut a deal or whatever to get their help. Could they tease you? Possibly. But remember, what you are doing is important, worth some effort, and maybe even some embarrassment. Almost any REAL friend is honored to be asked.

Next in line is the gift remembering. It comes in two forms. First is a size sheet. Keep it with your sheet of annual events. As she buys things, note mediums, larges, 10's, 12's, 14's, etc. And key words like petite or tall. When in doubt ask a store person. Cautions. All clothes vary in actual size from one manufacturer to the next. When buying, you want to ask if that line runs smaller or larger. Also, always keep the receipt. Plus you should be sensitive to weight changes. And, not finally, but the last one I am going to list, be careful not to buy something that is exactly the same as you saw her contribute to Goodwill last week.

If you have a good memory and are sensitive, you have it made. If not, write it down. Sounds simple; it is. Just remember, or don't forget to be sensitive. Log it, put it on the calendar, and oh yes, don't forget to look at the calendar.

The next part of gift remembering gets into hints. That is in the next chapter and also applies to other hints or things like going out or staying in. Hint gathering is neat and really a part of this whole process.

Before we leave this topic, we need to address those few who just have real trouble remembering. These are the men who forget where they put the memory-jogging list, or forgot to look at the calendar. This is the absent minded professor type. Possibly brilliant, but he is not the best in this area. If you are here, think about saying, "Honey, I really want to observe all of these occasions but I have a real problem remembering. If you could remind me it would help me be more romantic. And I want to be romantic for you." We are not scorekeeping or I would yell, "Good for this guy!" Actually that move isn't a bad idea for all of us.

5

Hint Gathering

o o o o o o o o o o o o o o o o o o o o o o o o o o o o o o o o o

"Ah, come on, just one little hint."

—*Heard wherever a wrapped present is not to be opened*
immediately.

Before I get into a world of hurt, I need to clear the air again. Many relationships don't need the hint stuff. Many can operate directly. "What do you want for Bastille Day, honey?" And so forth. Also, many women are more direct than to use indirect hints. This can vary from "If you really loved me you would…" or "I'd like this for a present."

In the process of gathering hints or signals, one must be cautious to understand what is really being communicated. That statement opens the door to cover the whole communication process, which is worth several books. Communication between men and women is different from communication between men and men, and between women and women. The main difference is that men tend to relay information while women process feelings. Yeah, yeah, yeah, there are tons of exceptions and this is not my area of expertise but bear with me for a thought or two.

Men will exchange information and opinion. Men visiting with men can be heard to say, "What do you think about those expansion teams?" "Where is the market going to go?" "I read an article in…." "Last week I heard a speech." "In my opinion," or "I think." Women visiting with other women are much more likely to be heard saying,

"Well, you can imagine how I felt after hearing that." "Tell me about it. I want to hear all about it." "I was so embarrassed." "How would you feel?" "Can you imagine…." And so on.

In addressing men/women communication, we have an opportunity to explore a classic problem common to all communication. What is heard is not always what is said. Let's give an example. She says, "Can you imagine, they put in a sprinkler system. That must have cost a bundle." In the male mind, that might be taken as a hint to get a sprinkler system. It could also be mistaken as a slam. "If you made enough, we could have that." Instead, the woman could be saying, "Sure, I'm jealous about what they have, that's why I mentioned it because unless I can talk it through and get my FEELINGS out, I will regret it."

This is a long way of making a simple point. Be sensitive to what is being communicated, not just what is being said. They may be different. How do you know the difference? No magic whatsoever. Experience laced with sensitivity. Of course, you can always ask, "What the _____ did you mean by that," or some other well-crafted phrase.

Well, now that you are sensitized, what do you do? First step is to raise your antenna. No, no, not the antenna you hear with. Sometimes you can be very difficult. Listen to what is being said and look for keys, key words and phrases that is. The following is a list of hint phrases.

Hint Phrases

- I have always wanted…

- I am looking for…

- That is just what I wanted, but I can't afford it right now…

- You know the sweater that Carol was wearing, I would look great in it but in blue…

- George did the nicest thing for Gracie…

- I shouldn't get this should I...?

- What would you think about...?

- Why don't we ever...

- You will never guess what I saw...

One more thought about hints. If she does not share hints, or you just have a rough time separating a real hint from general dialogue, ask. Ask her? Well, that's okay if you and she are comfortable with that. If not, ask her best friend. Women are usually very good at knowing what their women friends want or don't want. All you need to do is ask.

A Pitfall

There is one situation which merits exploration. Consider this exchange, "That was a great movie. I don't suppose there is any frozen yogurt place open now; we might as well go home. What do you want to do?" Caution, caution, oh person of male persuasion. She is *not asking* you what *you* want to do. She is *not saying* let's go home. She is *HINTING* for you to (1) think of the nearest frozen yogurt, and (2) give her permission to not go right home, but to go out of the way to have some yogurt. The antenna you have up has to be sensitive to what is meant—not just what is said.

Most women are very good at sending signals. But 'signals' is a male term. Women may use the word hints to describe the very same thing. The hints or signals come in many forms. Here are just a few:

- She says: "Isn't that the cutest outfit, I'd really love to have one like that."
  She means: "Birthday next month. If I'm getting clothes, that is a great idea."

- She says: "...and they went to that new restaurant, The Plentiful Pig, and just had the greatest time."
  She means: "Why don't we go there soon."

- She says: "...."

Now, we hear from Kamloops, British Columbia. "That's not too hard. Why can't they just say what they mean and be done with it? It's just not fair." Well, Kamloops, you possibly have a point, but you are also missing a point. Fair has nothing to do with it. Remember the saying, "All is fair in love and war." Part of what makes these creatures so loveable is this mysterious nature. I certainly don't pretend to understand it all. That's again why this is a book of guidelines and not rules.

◆   ◆   ◆

After doing "Why," "Who," and "How," we finally get to "What," to do in the next part.

PART IV
WHAT

6

The Little Things

"Life is made up, not of great sacrifices or duties, but of little things, in which smiles and kindness and small obligations, given habitually are what will preserve the heart and secure comfort."

—*Sir Humphrey Davey*

"Little drops of water, little grains of sand, made the mighty ocean and the pleasant land; so the little minutes, humble though they may be, make the might ages of eternity."

—*Mrs. Julia A. Fletcher Carney*

Many romantic intentions have died before they start because of size. We love to think of grandiose schemes and plots. The belief is that to do something grand is to really, really show our romantic side. The bigger the plans, the better. If I do this and that I will make the ultimate impression.

Certainly, there are times when the bold plan will carry the day. But when viewed in a strictly utilitarian sense, a constant stream of little things may do better and not strain time or budget as much. The ladies look for the little things and treasure them when done well.

Another perspective is to reflect upon the relationship. If you are building a relationship, you build one thing at a time and over time. A building made of bricks is made of many, many bricks, each one which is small in relation to the total building.

So little things make sense in a utilitarian sense and in a relationship sense. They also make sense in terms of expressing love. Sure love can well up and overflow. It can command all of your being for a while. It can consume you. But more likely, or more the case for most of the time, love is a continual presence, a constant state. This being true, our expressions of love should be reflective of this constancy. Frequent little things are much more likely to match this model of love.

One more piece on the big things. A big thing, all by itself, is likely to be suspicious. "What have you done that is so bad you need to do this?" Or, "What is it you want that causes this grand gesture?" If it is out of pattern, it raises questions. However, if you have built a relationship and pattern of little things, you have a foundation upon which the big gesture can ride with comfort.

One of the key concepts expressed in this book is that of nurture. If a gesture is nurturing, it is good. If it does not nurture, then something is wrong. A constant stream of little things is more nurturing than a sporadic big thing.

A good way to look at this is to think of the plant, as described in Chapter Two. Plants do best when they get frequent gentle applications of moisture. The exception may be the cactus, which will rot when over watered and prefers sparser and less frequent moisture. What kind of an image do you have when thinking of hugging a cactus? Not the most romantic. OK, ready for the list?

The Little Things

- Suggest staying home "just the two of you." You don't even need plans, just time together because you want to be together. Women love relationships. They love to feel wanted, not just in bed or behind the sink or as another paycheck in the home. They want to feel that you truly enjoy their company.

- Suggest going out. You may be observing that this point suggests the opposite of the above. The key is that you suggest something you don't normally do. Go out if the two of you are normally in and stay in if you are normally out. The message is that you wish to be with her. The difference in setting enhances that. Most important is that you are suggesting doing either with her.

- Comment on her hair, wardrobe.

- Pick and present a flower while walking. Giving a flower says, "I love you." It is a great way for those who get tongue tied to make a statement. Be careful not to violate park, state or federal laws. And be cautious not to pick an ugly weed or present a potential sneezing attack to an allergy sufferer.

- Send a card for no reason. Cards vary from full, detailed and elaborate messages to a very simple "thinking of you." Send a card from a business trip location. Pen in the card, "This meeting would be better if you were here." Send a card from the same town. Don't overdo or she will wonder what you are trying to hide.

- Take her hand. Hold it for a while or just give it a squeeze.

- If you have stuffed animals around the house, put one between the blanket and the pillow on her side. If you don't have one get one. If she says, "That's a childish thing to do," respond, "You bring out the kid in me."

- Cook dinner, unless you are a walking culinary crisis.

- Open doors for all woman. This costs so little and means so much. Your significant other will appreciate your opening the door for other women. She can say to herself, "See other female person, MY man is courteous." Whether that phrase is followed by the thought, "Eat your heart out," depends upon the individual. One caution is not to overdo. If you stay at the door while waiting for a lady to travel 15 more yards, your lady begins to wonder if you are more concerned with the other one than with her. Another caution is not to expect all women to respond the same way. Some will respond to your courteous action with a warm smile and will say, "Thank you." Others will completely ignore you and your actions. It is recommended that you resist the temptation to shout after them, "You're welcome," oozing sarcasm from every pore.

- If you go to work first, bring in the paper.

- Suggest talking. "Let's just talk instead of watching TV during dinner." This item should not be attempted if you have trouble talking. See the section on Comfort Zone in Chapter Fourteen. However, if talking with each other is comfortable, then suggesting it occasionally is a great move. Women love to talk and to be listened to. John Grey in *Men are from Mars and Women are from Venus* does a great treatment of conversation. Grey makes the point that talking out things is a part of a woman's process of sharing feelings. Be sure that you understand that this implies your role is to listen. Listen, not responding to each point or discuss or debate. Listen, Listen, Listen. If you can read the first few chapters of Grey's book, it is a real insight.

- Offer to do the dishes.

- Offer to do anything that she normally does and you normally don't do. You can say, "Here, let me do that. You always do that, I can take a turn."

- Do the dishes you have offered to do.

- Bring up a cup of tea or coffee while she is still in bed. This is a great one because it is highly appreciated, but does not commit to a full breakfast in bed. Some don't like to have breakfast in bed. Even if some do, there are many things that can go wrong. Everyone has a different routine. The routine may call for much to be done before even "thinking" about food. Others have very specific breakfast ideas. For example, a petite lady may only want tea and a piece of dry toast. To regale her with an omelet and hash browns smothered in country gravy will back fire.... Stay simple, the little things. By the way, a flower on a tray or resting on the saucer is great.

- Dry the dishes you have done.

- Put away the dishes you have dried.

- Hang up the towel you used to dry the dishes.

This is the longest list in the book, but probably also the most incomplete. The total list of little things is endless and often unique to each person. The real goal here is to express the true worth of little things and also raise the sensitivity to them.

It may be easy to challenge a number of the above by saying, "That's not a romantic gesture, that's just being kind." Great observation and right on. If a romantic gesture is nurturing, chances are it is kind. Is all kindness romantic? Possibly, but sometimes not. The point is that being kind is a major part of being romantic.

7

Flowers

"Flowers are love's truest language."

—*Park Benjamin*

To analyze charms of flowers is like dissecting music; it is one of those things which is far better to enjoy than to attempt fully to understand.

—*Henry Theodore Tuckerman*

Ah, the flower…. Truly, there is nothing else that can tug at the heart of a woman faster than a flower. God has given us prewritten poems in every flower. It is the language of love for those who cannot speak all that they feel.

I now hear someone from Newark saying, "OK, author person, enough poetic stuff, give me the when and where of flower." I guess this can be paraphrased into: "Let's get on with it," and so we shall.

The first point is that flowers follow the guidelines set out in previous chapters. Flowers are simple. The gesture of flowers is unmistakable. Even when flowers are given as a peace making gesture the message is, "I'm sorry," as well as "Will you forgive me?" The most powerful is the flower given for no apparent reason or no particular occasion. The "Just because…" flower. In fact a card saying, "Just because…" is not bad at all.

When to Give Flowers

Flowers are always, always, in order. However, there is some distinction between occasions and types of flowers. Probably the easiest is flowers for an occasion such as birthday, anniversary, congratulations, in hospital, etc. These are possibly obligatory situations but can be moments for romantic expressions. Normally, an arrangement from a florist best fits here. Talk to the florist. Most are very sensitive about what the flowers say and what impact they will have. Also, listen to your lady for impact. She will let you know what fits or what doesn't. Remember to take notes, mental or written.

The non-occasions become occasions with the gift of flowers. Some non-occasions are:

- Tomorrow is Tuesday.

- Returning from a trip.

- Just because…

- Beginning of spring—The first of May was celebrated with the giving of a May basket containing flowers, but not currently practiced. Maybe the mention here will revive the practice.

- Upon finishing a project or activity.

- Reaching a milestone. Pay off the mortgage—getting you first home, or the first brand new car.

- Getting a raise.

- And on and on.

Probably the most fun are the "Just because…" flowers. My wife, Peg, has her own job and becomes involved in activities just as I do. That makes both of us cherish and enjoy the time together that much more. It also allows me to get flowers and drive to where her office is, put them in her car, (I have a set of keys to her car) and depart without being seen. This is not done very often. It is just a special treat that is all the more special when it is least expected. It is fun just to show up with flowers or to have them at a table before you arrive at a restaurant or in a hotel room when on a vacation, or pick them on a walk.

What to Give and How

There is almost an endless variety in what to give and how. Keep in mind that the act of giving the flowers is probably more important than the flowers. A single wild flower on a walk can be more significant than a carload of orchids depending upon how it is done and the message and the feeling with it.

Fresh flowers usually have more feeling than plants. Plants are more utilitarian. They go on. Fresh flowers say, "Please accept this burst of beauty as a token of my surge of feelings for you." Do not give silk flowers. They can be beautiful, but they are fake. And when dealing the emotions, fake is dangerous.

I return, as I have done, and will do, to the single flower. I think we men have a notion that only a large thing is adequate to express *our* feelings. This comes from some old cave man type casting that says, "I provide, I provide a lot, I provide enough." If we follow this, then the question must be asked, "What is enough?" Aren't two dozen better than one dozen? Well what about three? The man tape is, "More is better." The woman tape is, "The thought counts." The single flower contains the thought just as well as a bunch. In fact, if we are talking gesture, the single flower may be better. Best of all, is a mix: sometimes a flower, sometimes a plant, sometimes a bouquet, and sometimes an arrangement.

Should you have a card? The answer is dependent upon what you are trying to say. Keep in mind that the flower itself is a message. The message begins, "I care, and I appreciate you." The message continues, "…and I want the beauty you are to me, to be complimented by this example of nature's beauty." That's a strong message. Add to it, or embellish if you wish, and, of course, be sensitive to what you love likes or doesn't. You may want to see the chapter on Words.

If you practice the flower art, you will find that having flowers delivered, brought, or left to be discovered are all viable. Surprise is important. There is something precious when a flower appears without being expected.

A special word about flowers for those who are not your wife. I give flowers to others, men and women, but mostly women. This can be beautiful, but make sure you are not sending the wrong message. If in doubt, leave this practice to the advanced romantic.

The real tragedy is the statement from a few women who have shared with me that they have never received flowers from anyone—not spouse, child, or colleague. That is really sad.

Next, please consider some special do's and don'ts about flowers.

Flower Do's

- Do ask florists for ideas, particularly if you don't have the feel.

- Do buy fresh flowers.

- Do ask for water pics. This is a little glass vial at the end of a stem, which will prolong the life of the flowers. Particularly ask for this if it will be several hours between purchase and presenting.

- Do check out fashions of the day before getting a corsage. Some ladies hate pin-ons, others hate wrist corsages, and many don't like corsages at all. *Best Bet*: ask a close friend of your lady what her preferences are and what color she will be wearing. When you ask, start with, "Would it be a good idea to…." If you start with, "I'm going to get Brunhilda a corsage…", you are not as open to the response that she may not like a corsage. Remember, her close friend may not want to hurt your feelings, so how you ask is important.

- Do cut off stems an inch or two from the bottom whenever stems have been out of water for a while. The bottom will dry and prevent water from traveling to the blossom. This will make a difference in the life of the flower. A rose, which does not open and just leans over the stem, typically does this because the stem is not carrying water. Incidentally, if you sense that this is happening, immerse the whole flower in water for 25 minutes. This may revive it. When cutting, cut under water, then immediately place in water.

- Do have a vase that fits the flowers. Use a narrow one for a single stem, a broad one for a bunch, etc. As elsewhere, the flowers and the vase should be in balance.

- Do use the plant food package often obtained with fresh flowers. If this is not available, put a bit of sugar in the water. Use warm water in the vase.

- Do ask for a few babies' breath to be part of your bouquet, particularly with roses, whether single or a bouquet. It may cost a bit more, but probably not much.

- Do keep in mind that different flowers may send different messages:

Lilies		Funeral
Roses		
	Red	Love
	White	Purity
	Yellow	Friendship
	Pink	Sweetheart

- Do listen for clues from your loved one. "Aren't those beautiful *so and so's*. I just love *so and so's*.

- Do send flowers by phone. You can now send flowers by calling 24 hours a day and using your plastic. The service charges are very nominal and the results are surprisingly good.

Flower Don'ts

- Don't always give flowers to say you are sorry and then expect them to all of a sudden have a romantic impact.

- Don't give silk flowers as a romantic gesture. They are great as a gift and nice to have, but not very romantic.

- Roses are particularly subject to bargains. A dozen roses for $5.00 is highly suspect. They may last 24 hours and never open. Consider a single quality rose which will slowly open and last for a week or more. The beauty of a quality single rose has much greater impact than almost anything else.

- Don't give the same thing every time. Part of the flower ceremony is surprise. Of course, there is an exception where the relationship is mature and the same thing is a tradition.

- Don't overdo. Gestures that happen too often become habit and lose the edge of impact that a surprise has.

8

Words

"Such as the words are, such will thy affections be esteemed; and such will thy deeds be as thy affections; and such thy life as thy deeds."

—*Socrates*

"My words fly up, my thoughts remain below; words, without thoughts, never go to leave."

—*William Shakespeare*

Words are very much like people. They come in all shapes and sizes. They have a wide range of personalities and intensities. They have various degrees of color and shading. And they can get you into trouble as well as aid your cause.

Sweetheart can be very affectionate; it can also be delivered with sarcasm dripping from each letter. Another good one is *honey*. While *honey* is a term of endearment for many, it is a demeaning sexist term in other situations. Picture your image of the classic dirty old man addressing an attractive, just out of teller training with, "Hey, *honey*, how ya fixed for money?"

Calling my wife "Love" is an OK greeting. However, I can use the same greeting on someone I see walking down the block and can get into trouble. In still another setting, this same term is all right for use with a total stranger. Picture yourself going into an English pub. The woman behind the counter may very easily say, "What will you have, Love?" By the way, that is spelled, "What'll you have, LUV?" This may remind us of George Bernard Shaw's statement, "The United States and Great Britain are two great nations separated by a common language."

The point of this introduction is that the words themselves are not as important as the context. Some words fit the person using them and the person receiving them. They may also fit or not fit the situation, moment or location. The examples and lists which follow may not fit exactly what you want to say, when you want to say it, etc. As with everything else, "Use Appropriately."

Appropriate Use of Words

Just to keep things simple; if it works, it is appropriate. If it does not work, then it must have been inappropriate. With that absolutely brilliant statement, a guy from New Haven, Connecticut, asks, "Is that all there is? Is that the secret to life and if so, why do I need this book?" A well structured set of queries. They deserve a response.

A word oriented romantic gesture, such as, "I love you," should evoke a positive response. The response can be a smile, a reply such as "I love you, too," or just a bit of inner well being. If it engenders a negative feeling, a frown, or some other negative response, you have probably said the wrong thing to the wrong person, or at the wrong time, in the wrong place, or for the wrong reason. It's as simple as that.

Bangor, Maine, says, "Simple, my posterior. Communication is never that simple." Bangor is right. Communication is not that simple. But then this is a chapter on *words*—not a study of communication. Communication between persons, particularly a man person and a woman person, is an art, science and mystery all in one. The points in this guide are part of that communication but must be applied with the understanding of the who, what, when, where, and why context of the relationship.

Certainly, communication is a broad topic. It covers practically all of the interaction between humans. Some is verbal, some is not. In a sense, all of the gestures in this book are a form of communications. The reference to words is, too, a part of communication. Words are a very important part, but just a part.

Since communication with words is such a large, large part of communication, it is appropriate to take a leap at defining some categories. To this end, we will treat words under the categories of Affection, Adoration, Apology, Appreciation, and Affirmation.

Affection

"Our sweetest experiences of affection are meant to point us to that realm which is the real and endless home of the heart."

—Henry Ward Beecher

The word affection brings images of softness. It is not a word of passion. Adjectives often associated with affection are "mild" or "gentle." Of all the word categories in this chapter, affection is the most comparable to the gentle rain nurturing a plant.

Some phrases are definitely affectionate. Examples would include, "You're sweet/nice," or "I like being with you." Others are on the border. The term, "I love you," can be very affectionate, very gentle. In a different context, the same phrase is full of passion. Therefore, the use or context of words or phrases is just as important as the word or words used.

Affection is nurturing. Affection is gentle and tender. Since it is like a gentle rain, it can occur often. You may show love by showering your lover with affection.

Affection is treated here as a word or phrase. Affection is also associated with touching. A squeeze of the hand, a hug, a pat on the arm, a stroke of the hair are all gestures of affection. Note that they are also mild, soft, tender, and gentle.

Affection is one of the areas where expression need not be restricted to your special love. Sharing a hug or phrase with family members or close friends, both male and female, is an often-encountered experience. Just make sure that you have direct or implied acceptance so that your gesture is not mistaken.

Affection Statements

- Hi, cutie.

- You look good in that.

- I feel good being with you.

- Buckle up! I don't want anything to happen to you.

- I love it when I'm near you.

- You are the prettiest at this party. No question.

- I love the way your nose turns up.

- If you wear that perfume again, I will not be responsible for my actions. (Hints at passion, but still affectionate.)

- You hands are so soft.

Appreciation

"You will find poetry nowhere unless you bring some with you."

—Joubert

The quotation above can be modified into "Appreciation of another will allow you to be appreciated." Think of this as another view of the Golden Rule or as a version of the giver being blessed more than the receiver of a gift.

These references can be twisted into a selfish pattern by observing that if you want to get, then give. It often works, but not with the best of motives. The more pure view of appreciation is based on love and simply is an expression of one's feelings without thought of reward.

Desire for appreciation is a most universal and basic need. We all want to be appreciated for what we do and for who we are. Don't we puff up after the boss has said, "good job," or a hostess says, "I'm glad you're here." Of course we do.

While we cherish these situations which are external to our home, we often neglect to enjoy that climate at home. Maybe it's easy to take appreciation for granted at home. "Of course, I appreciate what she does. I married her, didn't I?" Bravo, Mr. Hardcase, you have just won a prize for being out of touch. Marriage is a contract to continue to love and cherish, not a rescue.

Many studies have been done on the need humans have to be touched. This need begins at birth and continues throughout life. Think of a word of appreciation just like a word of affection, as a touch, necessary as a part of life, necessary as a part of nurture.

Appreciation is broader than the romantic. It is an expression, which applies to all of our relationships. Try, for an exercise, to think of something to appreciate in each person you are with or close to for the next day or week. I will guarantee that you will be surprised at how much there is. Even the grumpiest SOB at work does something that is appreciable. Try it. Now, after observing what is appreciated, begin to say so. Start slow and cautiously. After all, you don't want your cohorts to conclude that you have finally flipped out. As you do this, you are bound to get a, "Why, thank you. It's so nice of you to notice." Now reflect on the quotation that began this part of the chapter, "You will find poetry nowhere unless you bring some with you." (Joubert). Appreciation begets appreciation.

One would think that if this is true, that appreciation should flow and flower in a relationship of love, yet it often doesn't flourish where it should. Even where appreciation is present, it may not be spoken, may not be conveyed. We assume. We take for granted. How sad.

But it is never too late. Appreciation is always appreciated. It is appreciated most when timely, but is always appreciated. The guideline is always to consider where you have been and are coming from and ease into it. If you are an appreciative person, then do a bit more. If you are not very appreciative, or don't verbalize it, begin by spending some time looking for things to appreciate.

The following list of appreciation statements may help.

Appreciation Statements

- Thank you.

- I like it when you…

- You look nice tonight.

- I like that dress.

- Thanks for fixing that dish for dinner.

- I love you.

- I'm glad that I married you.

- You are fun to be with.

- I like spending time with you.

- I appreciate you.

- Twenty years of marriage and you are still my girlfriend.

- I love you, but you are also my best friend.

- That's a great idea.

You have probably noticed that the affection and appreciation statements are close and in some ways the same. Yes, they are very similar word categories. And statement of affection can be appreciating. Also, an appreciation statement can be affectionate. The categories are all subject to some overlap, but particularly these two.

Adoration

Believe me, if all those endearing young charms
Which I gaze on so fondly today,
Were to change by tomorrow and fleet in my arms,
Like fairy gifts fading away,
Thou wouldest still be adored as this moment thou art,
Let thy loveliness fade as it will,
And around the dear ruin each wish of my heart
Would entwine itself verdantly still.

—Thomas Moore

A simple way to think of adoration is to view it as appreciation multiplied by love. Adoration is found in the, "I can't help it. I'm lost in love," level of feeling. In youth, it is the head over heels feeling, the nothing else matters feeling. In maturity, it is looking at your one and only and just *feeling* a depth of love, warmth, and tenderness that is very special. As sexual feelings range from longing to passion, so the *heart feelings* can range from affection to adoration.

In the appreciation section there was a suggestion that appreciation can be found if looked for. Adoration is felt or not felt. If it is not felt, work on the other romantic gestures. If it is felt, express it.

<u>Adoration Statements</u>

- I truly love you.

- I cannot imagine life without you.

- You are very precious to me.

- You make life worthwhile.

- I cherish you.

- I adore you.

Adoration can mean placing upon a pedestal, but doesn't need to take that course. It is primarily a depth of feeling. As such it is powerful. Most of the impact of the above phrases is the spirit of communication. These are special words for that special person at a special time or place but most important expressed with special feeling.

Some of you may have a hard time here. If you really want to be cautious and you really feel adoration, you could try, "I know I don't say much about how I feel, but I do adore you." As always, be yourself.

Apology

"I won't apologize for the quotation not being here because it is in the fourth paragraph below."

—John P. Borden

It is impossible to go through life without making a mistake here and there. Some of our goofs fade into the night with no one affected. Those, which affect others, may present opportunities for apology. If something is done wrong and not corrected or acknowledged as wrong, the thing can fester and grow to be quite ugly. If it is acknowledged as a wrong and some expression of sorrow or regret expressed, the wrong falls away faster and does not accrue the interest of avoidance. This is not to say that there are not some wrongs, which are just too big to forgive and forget. But for the most part, our mistakes are forgivable and forgettable. And to forgive and forget begins with an apology.

The apology can and should express two thoughts. The first is the event and the expression that the event was wrong, a mistake, a stupid, an awkward, an inappropriate or whatever. The second area of expression is the change of heart, which says, "I will try not to do that again."

Expression of this second thought can be through words or the way you express them. If your apology is expressing the first thought only, it seems to be saying that you are sorry you were caught more than sorry for the event.

As with appreciation, the apology fits into all of our interactions—not just the romantic. Also, as with appreciation, there is no way for us to retain or maintain a relationship of romance if we do not address these simple communications of feelings.

The apology is sometimes viewed as weakness. Even as respected an author as Ralph Waldo Emerson wrote, *"No sensible person ever makes an apology."* Well, I'm afraid I disagree strongly with Mr. Emerson. It takes courage and strength to say, "I goofed, I blew it." To hide our mistakes, to ignore them, to hope no one will find out is quite childish and usually results in more damage than necessary or appropriate. The truly manly man acknowledges mistakes, wrongs, etc. and seeks forgiveness with apology.

Apology Statements

- I'm sorry.

- I misjudged that, I'm sorry.

- I goofed.

- I blew it.

- I screwed up.

- I made a mistake when I…

- I didn't mean to, but I did.

Notice that all of the statements begin with the personal pronoun, "I'. This is one area where the over abundance of the "I" word is OK. You are owning up to your situation and claiming responsibility.

A word of caution is appropriate. Watch carefully for the distinction between apology and passing the blame back. Take for example, "I would have been on time if it were not for,...I'm sorry." This is not apology, but blaming and self-justification. In general, the inclusion of a blame phrase negates the apology. Some of us do this frequently and possible unconsciously. Listen to how you handle apology.

Affirmation

"We live in a world which is full of misery and ignorance, and the plain duty of each and all of us is to try to make the little course he can influence somewhat less miserable and somewhat less ignorant than it was before he entered it."

—Thomas H. Huxley

Affirmation is one of the areas of greatest need in communication. All of us need to know that we are okay, needed, valued, important and fitting into the greater scheme of things.... Our latest caller is from Sulphur, Oklahoma, and remarks, "Hey, Author Person, this sounds a bit like approval or appreciation. What gives? What is the difference?"

Great observation. Try this out. All of us need to feel okay as a person. We need validation. This is a formal term, but also can work in our layman context. Validation is the action that says I am okay, I am worthwhile, I am important, and I am needed, and so on. Yes, Sulfur, the affirmation is a form of communication like appreciation. Appreciation is broader with affirmation linked to the concept of validation.

Some persons seem to carry a natural affirmation. You see these folks and observe that they have everything all together and probably never had a problem in their life. Wrong. No one has escaped the need to have said to them, "Okay...That's okay. You're okay. The person who seems all together may be putting on a mask or may already be bathed in affirmation.

For most of us, there is always a little nagging doubt about what we are doing and whether we are truly valued or truly loved. This being the case, we are all in need of validation or affirmation. And, if we all need something like this, where do we go? To our lover, our friend, our partner, our spouse, of course. This is where we go first. This is also where we should go. Many have created problems by seeking affirmation outside their prime relationships.

For a moment, let us look at the other side. Unfortunately, lack of affirmation or the classic put down is very often found in relationships. Such phrases as:

- You're no good.

- Why did I marry you?

- I could have done…if it weren't for you.

These are deadly missiles which directly attack self worth. This is one area where we won't have a list of don'ts because the don'ts are phrases like those above and not healthy at all. As observed before, if it doesn't nurture, don't do it.

So affirmation is needed and valued. Don't I need it also? Of course, we all need affirmation. Many of us get affirmation from our buddies. Men seek it from other men and the women seek it from other women. If that's true, should not affirmation also come from you, the significant other? Absolutely. In fact, affirmation from you is more important than from anyone else.

One of the areas of life where we need affirmation is in what we do, our work. A truck driver can say that his job is important because persons would not get what his truck is carrying if he did not drive. His driving is important and he therefore is also important. That's fairly clear. The one who gets most into trouble is housewife and mother.

I personally and totally believe that running a home and raising a family is a highly important role and terribly undervalued by our society. The results can be seen in the obvious shift in family values being directly correlated with time spent parenting. Since most of the parenting time is from the woman, the child rearing profession is essentially in the female camp. It is critically important, yet very threatened in our society.

Now that the point is raised, let's do something with it. What phrases do we use when we are describing the role of a woman who is rearing and homemaking? Do we say she is doing a great job as a guiding force for our children and keeps a great home? Or do we say, "Oh, she's just a homemaker." One is affirming, one is not.

Men, this point is important and is pivotal. If we, as men, truly respect the homemaker and/or child-rearing role, we can and should affirm it. If we affirm that role, we are on our way to other affirming. If we cannot affirm that role, we probably have trouble with other affirmations. The great test here is for the male person to take over the role for a few days or a week. Some could, but most would have a rougher time than they would expect.

One last note before we get into our list. Remember the Golden Retriever getting a rose as an anniversary present? Lost on the dog, right? Well, now try saying to the dog, "Good dog." You have affirmed. What is the result? A wagging tail. "Come on now," someone says, "The dog doesn't speak English. But the dog does understand the owner paying attention and taking time with the dog, which AFFIRMS the dog's place, importance, well being and feeling needed.

Affirming Statements

• I'm glad you are here.

• You do…well.

• I don't know how you do it, but….

• I don't know what I would do without you.

• We couldn't be where we are without your special touch.

• You are a treasure.

- I would be nothing without you.

- You are very important in my life.

Write it—Say it

Either writing it or saying it can convey almost everything covered in this chapter. Is there any best way? Yes, and no. Yes, there may be a time, place and way for you to best use any of these words. But, no, there is nothing that says my way is best for you and yours is best for me. This is a great place for expression. "Do you own thing." Or better, "Do your own thing, your nurturing thing."

Part of doing your own thing is to be comfortable. If you never write notes, maybe saying what you want to communicate is best. By the same token, some have a very difficult time expressing what they feel verbally. For them, penning a word or two in the privacy of their own space is preferable. Keep in mind that we are all different. Use your uniqueness to your advantage.

9

Chivalry

"The age of chivalry is never past, so long as there is a wrong left unredressed on earth."

—*Charles Kingsley*

Contrary to the belief of many, chivalry is not dead. It is less than flourishing, but it is not dead.

No one has called in yet, but if they did, the issue might be to question the connection between chivalry and romantic gestures. Chivalry describes a code of conduct which grew out of the medieval times when knights met around round tables, slew dragons, and most importantly, rescued maidens. In a broad sense, chivalry governed the interaction between all persons, not just men and women. It was, and is, based on the simple notions of protect the weak, be truthful and honest, honor your word, be kind to all except when righting a wrong.

The fit with romantic gestures is that of decent, proper, or good behavior. Certainly, this applies when dealing directly with your significant other. But it also applies to dealing with others. Your significant other will take pride in your being gallant, or courteous, or thoughtful to others.

An important aspect of considering chivalrous behavior is to be careful to recognize that times have changed. What was great 400 to 600 years ago may not apply well today. A case in point is dragons. You just don't see as many dragons as you used to. Ain't it a shame.

Well, what's a fellow to do if he wants to go on a quest and there are no more dragons? Maybe dragons do exist, but in a different form. They are now in the form of a stupid ordinance that needs to be repealed, or the challenge to tough out working for a bad boss, or coming to the defense of a friend or neighbor unjustly accused by the rumor mill. It's too bad that that's what dragons are today. They were probably more fun in medieval times.

Another chivalrous practice which has changed is walking on the street side of a lady. This practice allegedly began in merry old England when houses were built with the second floor hanging our several feet beyond the first floor. In those times, there was no plumbing and no garbage collection. Disposal consisted of dumping your s...stuff out the second story window. This practice could result in a passer-by being decorated with your toss. Of course, one would not want the lady to get splattered, and that meant that the gentleman would take the position most likely to get it. This practice might also explain the broad rimmed hats men used to wear.

Today we have indoor plumbing, and, except for strikes, fairly regular garbage collection. As a result, the practice is not as religiously followed as it once was. In fact, the practice is now reversed, at least in the city. Should you be strolling down the street in the city of your choice, the gentleman should walk on the inside. This is in order to intercept any problems coming from the alley. If it sounds like the gentleman's role is to intercept garbage from overhead or from the side, you are right. Ain't manhood great!!

Another quaint custom is to offer your lady your hand when she alights from the carriage, (I mean car) or offer her your arm to escort her inside and so on. The arm or hand you extend is your left. Why you ask? To keep your sword hand free, of course.

While some of the practices have changed, the intention and spirit of chivalry is still alive, at least in part. It is still polite to open the door for someone, or let someone go first, or help someone with luggage in the overhead bin in an airplane. Notice that all of these examples apply to men and women. Again, the idea is just being thoughtful. Does that count as a romantic gesture? It does, if the other party is a romantic party.

Like other gestures, the chivalrous ones can be overdone or are not always appropriate. Remember who, what, where, when, and why. If they are not natural for you, try a few and see what happens. Remember that the goal is to express and enhance romance—not to showboat or score keep, or to make your partner uncomfortable.

One of my favorites is the man who laments, "I'd love to be a gentleman if I could only find a woman who is a lady." It is true that some women don't know how to graciously accept acts of chivalry, just as some men don't know how to extend acts of chivalry. These hints may not be comfortable to them, either of them.

Be sensitive to your partner's expectations. Observe what others do. Ask, "Do you want me to open the door?" If you get, "Thank you." You have learned that this is positively received. If the response is "No," or "Why," or "What's the matter with you?" you have also learned something. By the way, a good comeback is, "Oh, I saw it done in the movies."

So armed with this discussion on chivalry, you are now ready for a list of do's and don'ts. Pick what suits your relationship.

CHIVALRY DO'S

- Open car doors. (I heard of one couple having a spat. The lady went to the car and waited to have the door opened for her. The "gentleman," who was angry and preoccupied, went to his side, opened his door, got in, started the car and drove off, assuming his partner had gotten in by herself. This did not cool things off.)

- Allow women to go first. Exception, revolving doors. When approaching the door the man should go first to supply the power. If you are not sure, then say, "Let me get this started." Another exception is the elevator. If you are one of the last on, and it's a relatively full car, get off first and out of the way rather than force her and others to maneuver around you.

- When something is dropped, say, "Let me," and then pick it up. Not to say, "Let me," may invite the knocking of heads as both go after the treasure.

- Ask if you are unsure, "May I open the door?" This will give you immediate feedback.

- Offer to help with packages, luggage.

- Let the lady order first.

CHIVALRY DON'TS

- Don't object to a lady picking up a tab. It is now fashionable to share. Equality tempers chivalry.

- Don't start eating until all are served. Exception, waiting for a special order or a large group to be served. Ask, "May we go ahead," or wait until someone says, "Please, go ahead."

- Don't start eating until the hostess has begun or until another lady has begun, or either has placed the appropriate piece of silver on the plate. (For more, see a handbook on etiquette, which is heavily connected to chivalry.)

- Don't use bodily functions or sounds as a source of humor. I don't like it even with just the men. I sense that most men laugh only to avoid offending the person sticking out their finger to be pulled.

- Don't verbally put down your partner, even if others are doing it. For that matter, don't put anyone down.

Private vs. Public

Some of the words which are often connected with chivalry are *honor* and *gallantry*. These suggest a code of conduct, a way to behave. The point is made throughout the book that gesturing should be nurturing. In order to behave properly and be nurturing, one observes that some gestures are best in private and some in public. Many of the gestures listed above are from public occasions.... However....

For the most part, romantic gestures are private matters. Certainly sex and touching are private, or should be. It is very awkward to see a couple expressing intimacy in public. At least it is for me and I believe for many others. An argument can be made for almost all other gestures that privacy should be the rule.

Of course, all rules have their exceptions. There are times when flowers delivered to the work place are special. For that matter, flowers at the hairdresser waiting for your love are OK also. You get the idea. As with all other gestures, the test is whether the gesture works and is nurturing. If the message is "Here, rest of the world, see how great I am in buying her flowers," then you have failed. On the other hand, if the message is, "I don't want to embarrass you, but I want to share with others how much you are loved," then you have captured the idea.

10

Gifts and Presents

"Every gift, though it be small, is in reality great if given with affection."

—Pindar

It is expected that everyone is aware of the appropriateness of gifts on certain occasions. Occasions where gifts are almost mandatory are:

Birthdays
Christmas/Hanukkah
Anniversary
Mother's Day
Valentines Day

The type and size of gifts on those occasions is between the parties in the relationship. The romantic side of this is that different gifts send different messages. The delivery of a new washer and dryer on the 25th wedding anniversary says, "Our relationship is sturdy, clean and utilitarian, keep up the good work...." That's not very loving. Of course, if she said, "I really want a washer and dryer," then that's what you should consider. However, you could tape some theater tickets to the dryer door or have some flowers inside or something to convey a bit of warmth, tenderness, affection and all those other things we have been discussing.

Similar points can be made for gifts of vacuum cleaners, toasters, blenders and so on. The point is to separate utilitarian items from romantic. With that last sentence, we get a call from Blacksburg, Virginia, from a gentleman who observes that Father's Day advertising is almost exclusively lawn and garden tools, power tools and all other tools for working around the house. His question is how does this fit with a non-utilitarian observation made above. Well, I think we have something here. Mother's Day is dining out, jewelry, perfume, etc. Father's Day is tools, tools, and more tools. Maybe our society needs to have some romance flow in both directions. Maybe men enjoy romantic attention also. What do you say men? You do enjoy it a bit, don't you? Maybe we need to tell the ladies that we do enjoy a bit of romantic gesturing, probably not as much. Just a bit here and a bit there.

Well, what about other times? Certainly flowers are gifts and we have covered that. The next item is words as found on cards. Some people are card people, some are not. This is an area of definite bias. A non-card person will appreciate a card once in a while. A card person can also appreciate a card but can go ballistic if a card is forgotten. Card persons appreciate cards on all occasions for which the card companies have elected to print cards. Make sure you do these. The key is to send or give a card on some occasions which are not occasions. Send a card from a conference. Send one from downtown even though you live 10 miles away in the suburbs. Send an anniversary card on the first anniversary of planting a new tree and most important, send a "Just because" card, a "Thinking of you" card. The difference is that the card for some is an obligation and has a negative impact if not sent, while for the other, cards sent for no specific occasion can be nothing but romantic.

When you select cards, be sensitive to what your partner enjoys. Some cards have lengthy poems that are great if that's what you like. Some are humorous and that can be appreciated. Be a bit cautious with humor it can be overly sarcastic or demeaning. At times, the best cards are blank on the inside, allowing you the opportunity to express your own thoughts. (PSSST, you can also use one of the many phrases in this book as totally your own. See chapter on Words.)

What kinds of gifts make good romantic gestures in addition to flowers and not washers and dryers? Almost anything if it says, "I care, I appreciate you, I thought of you, I love you."

Clothing is always appropriate. My last clothing purchase for Peg was on a trip to a conference at a resort. She couldn't join me and I know she wanted to be there. Peg doesn't expect a gift from each trip. However, she does enjoy it when I return with a surprise. On this occasion, I was going through several of the resort type shops, looking for the right thing. At one stand, I saw a shirt and knew I had to get it for her. It was among all the artsy, craftsy things, which are everywhere. It was a plain tee shirt, but had gold angels coming out of the pocket and over a small area around the pocket. It came rolled up, tied with a ribbon, with a little card, and was titled, "A Pocketful of Angels." It was not as expensive as some other gifts, but Peg loves angels. She has a small collection and reads about them. She and I both believe in angels (not that that is important to you.) What is important was that this gift said, "I love you and I know you love angels and I took some extra time to find a very personal and special gift for you because you are special to me...." She loved that gift more than most.

How do you find an angel shirt for your lady? First step is to be sensitive to what she likes and wants. When you are shopping together, don't just stare off in space.... Observe. What does she say is cute? Lock on when she says, "I'd really love that sometime." Remember also to take notes as to sizes, etc. Over time you could get fairly good at that and advance to knowing she loves (color), loves (sleeved vs. sleeveless), loves (low or high necklines), how long, short or medium skirt length and so on. Remember to keep receipts in case it doesn't fit. Also, pay close attention to what stores she likes. If she is a Talbot's person and wants to exchange, she will be happy to exchange the Talbot's item because she has a chance to get something else from a store where she likes to shop.

Clothing is used as an example because it is always appropriate and because it has more do's and don'ts. Other gifts are basically dependent upon her likes and dislikes. Candy, books, puzzles, glass, brass, another piece in her collection of whatever, tickets to events. Again, observe and remember to record what does she oohs and ahhs over when shopping.

There is an almost final thought on gifts for those for whom buying is difficult. Some persons have everything, or appear to, or are very picky. Another group presents a similar problem. Those are the persons who are simplifying life. Peg and I fit into that category. Our children are grown and we are cleaning and clearing out stuff. Stuff is not as important as it used to be. That creates a problem when giving. Our solution is to make some of the gifts to each other contributions to one of the charities we support. This is a very satisfying gesture for each of us. This may not work for all, but it is worth discussing with your partner. Remember things change over time. You need to be sensitive to those changes in and with each other.

A final thought on non-gift gifts. A great gift is time. Drop your love a note or E-mail, if you are so inclined. Another approach is to get on your computer and design a gift certificate. In it say, "Because ___(fill in the blank)_ I hereby give to you...." The gift can be a night of her not washing dishes, a day where she decides what you both will do, a dinner at that place you have never been, a day trip to a nice place that you have heard of, or a promise to do a project that you have been planning by a stated date, and more. If you do the night of not doing dishes, please remember that the gift is not letting them sit and soak over night, but doing them.

GIFTS AND PRESENTS DO'S

- Do make gifts personal, nurturing and loving whenever possible.

- Do give gifts at non-occasion times. In other words, make you own occasions.

- Do be sensitive to what she likes, her sizes, what styles she favors, what store she enjoys.

- Do be sensitive to cards.

- Do think of time as a gift.

- Do keep receipts

- Do splurge occasionally for professional gift-wrapping.

- Do be sensitive to when and how a gift is presented.

GIFTS AND PRESENTS DON'TS

- Don't buy appliances as a romantic gift.

- Don't buy from a store that has a bad return policy.

- Don't toss receipts.

- Don't leave the price tag on the gift.

- Don't give the same thing all the time.

Unique Gifts

There are times when it is appropriate to express a special thought toward that special person. While all the gestures can be special and are, they may not always be enough. Enough here is not in the quantity or quality sense. Enough here is used in the unique sense.

By definition, a unique gesture is not one that is done frequently. A unique gift is only unique if it is seldom given, even a once only situation.

You will observe that the thoughts that are embodied here are similar to those in the Chapter on Advanced Topics. Please note that actions and gifts that are advanced or unique need to have a foundation of regular gestures and attention against which the advanced or unique becomes a spice, not a shock. Advanced topics are later; here we are dealing with gifts. As always, make sure that the gift is nurturing and make sure it is consistent with the desires of the receiver and with the relationship.

A Tree

Giving a tree is a very special expression. This is not the tree that you buy from the nursery to plant in your back yard. No, we are describing a tree given to a public garden, park, school, zoo, or church. We are describing a tree with a plaque with the name of your special person. An extension of this is a tree in memory of a loved one she has lost.

A tree is truly a gift which keeps on giving. It is a living temple to your relationship. It is a declaration of beauty. It grows as your relationship grows. It is alive as your love is alive. It supports life in providing oxygen for us all and a home for some feathered and furry friends.

An Animal at the Zoo

Speaking of feathered and furry friends brings us to the next unique gift idea. Adopt an animal at the zoo. Most zoos have discovered this is an excellent additional funding source. For an unusual gift, you can actually adopt one of the animals or a specific animal. The cost is variable, depending upon the type of animal. It takes more to feed a hippopotamus than a gray fox.

Most women and many couples have a favorite animal. My wife likes bears. For a long time, we had an extensive collection of stuffed, cuddly bears around the house. We still have a few. I haven't done the zoo adoption yet, but bear with me. I may.

Adoption is based on an annual fee so that you can discontinue if that gesture has lost its appeal. On the other hand, you may enjoy the idea so much that you adopt more. Another benefit of this kind of gift is the ongoing opportunity to allow the gesture to reinforce itself by visiting your adopted animal periodically or regularly. "Honey, I was just thinking, you know it's been a while since we have seen our adopted hippo. Let's get a group together to go see her. Or better yet, just you and me."

A Star

Every now and again, there are ads for the purchase of a star. There are literally billions and billions of stars. Some enterprising soul has hit on the idea of naming the unnamed stars after persons. The service is a legitimate registration of the star in you loved one's name with a certificate and directions to locate your star.

In actual practice, you may need a very powerful telescope to find your star. I can assure you that it takes not only expensive equipment, but also training and expertise to locate specific stars. For most of us-who cares? You stand outside on the lawn or on the deck and say, "Look, I can see it. It's about this high from the horizon and about this much this side of North. See it? It's winking at you. That's your star honey." And for crying out loud, kiss her right there and then....

A Brick

A down to earth gift is the commemorative brick. For sure these are available at Disney World. There you can buy a commemorative brick which becomes part of the walkway around the Seven Seas Lagoon. For your purchase, you get a location finder and an excuse for a really great trip.

Other brick opportunities are available. I believe there is a yellow brick road in Kansas. Look also for river walks or projects reusing old brick structures, etc. Some organizations such as churches, hospitals, libraries and such use commemorative bricks as a source of fund raising or donation.

Donations

As mentioned earlier in this chapter, some persons have more than enough stuff. Some persons don't like stuff or want to limit stuff. For these folks, a donation might just fit the bill. It is a gift which can make you feel good, can significantly help some others and will not take up shelf space. Some couples we know are doing this more and more. Of course, you want to be sensitive to what cause or group your special someone holds dear.

A side benefit of this may be the discovery of a cause you both like to foster. This is a source of some possibly great sharing time together.

A Coupon Book

There are two thoughts here. One is to purchase one of the entertainment coupon books. This is presented tongue-in-cheek because this gift could backfire. If you are perceived as a cheapskate, then it may backfire. "You don't want to take me out unless you can do it on a discount." If done well, it can represent an opportunity for you to go out together, a lot.

The other kind of coupon book is one you can make up yourself. Earlier in the chapter, mention was made of printing up a computer page that presents a gift of time, such as doing the dishes one night. Take the idea further and make up a book of such coupons. Use clip art and go for it. Here is a list of coupon ideas.

Coupon Gifts from You

- One night of doing the dishes

- One visit to your mother's without…

- A dinner for two at home. I'll cook.

- A night at that Bed and Breakfast we saw at the lake.

- One day of painting the hallway

- Digging up the old garden plot

- An evening of dancing—I'll even dance.

- Your choice of opera or ballet—I won't yawn.

- Next movie is your choice

- I'll take a day off to help spring clean

- Weekend at any romantic place within 200 miles

- A dinner at the Ritz

- Two hours in the park

- A month of hanging up my clothes

This list can get quite long. It makes sense to design your own. This is very individual and unique.

Radio Request

The last gift mentioned is a radio request. You know, "This one is for cutie from monster man." This is a small, simple thing but may fit. The greatest problem could be that of listening to the program at the right time.

Presenting Unique Gifts

The presentation of the gift can be as important as the gift. If the gift is truly unique, it is worth a little extra to make the uniqueness come through. You want the uniqueness to have an impact. If you just give an envelope and say here is something for you, the gift speaks for itself. On the other hand, if you go out to dinner and then say the nice things that you like to say and she likes to hear and then give the gift, the impact is multiplied. It somehow is like saying that the sum of the parts is greater than the whole. If the dinner is one point and the gift one point, the two together are three points. Excuse the scorekeeping; it is only to make a point. That point is that the memory takes combinations of gestures and multiplies the sweetness, depth, and remembrance of the occasion.

11

Touching

"Upon thy cheek I lay this zealous kiss, as seal to the indenture of my love."

—*William Shakespeare*

All persons not only enjoy but also need to be touched by others. The act of touching can convey tenderness, affection, acceptance, understanding, sympathy and love. Touching can convey all of the thoughts and feelings conveyed by words.

A note of caution before we proceed. Anyone looking for the secrets of erotic touching best look elsewhere. Certainly romantic touching can lead partners to want greater intimacy and passion. The emphasis here is on gestures and nurturing, not on campaigning and conquering.

Another caution is that individuals do vary in their touchability index. The touchability index is non-scientific measurement of the receptivity of the subject person to touching from all sources. The index has yet to go through rigorous, or in fact, any testing whatsoever. It is not mentioned in any literature. The whole idea of a touchability index is to express that some persons love to touch and be touched all the time and involve all other persons. Examples are frequently found in large families and some European cultures. Others avoid touching or seem to. And, of course, there are an infinite number of points in between these extremes. The objective is not to argue or discuss the right, wrong, or wellness of any point on the index. The objective is to realize that where the persons are on the index scale is important to them and needs to be part of determining the nature and form of touching to represent a nurturing gesture versus an intrusion.

Hand to Hand

The hand is our main touching tool and the best place to start. The beginning is not holding hands, but just touching. Patting the hand or giving the hand a gentle squeeze is a great start.

Holding hands is a great romantic gesture. We occasionally hold hands while walking. More than once a neighbor has commented that they think it is so great to see a couple walking with hands united. And, of course, there are the movies.

Hugs

Next comes "hugs." Hugs can be shared with lovers, friends, and companions. The form varies widely. On one extreme, you have the hand squeeze where you take the upper arms in you hands and squeeze. You may draw the intended person forward but not with contact. Then there is the "A" frame hug where you do an arm squeeze, but touch cheeks. So, there you are with your feet widely apart from each other, but cheeks touching. My favorite is following the example of our bear friends. A few reject that form, most tolerate it, and a fair number relish it. Oh, by the way, hugging the other men is okay. Not all admit it, but most enjoy sharing a brief hug.

As always, you need to be sensitive to the other person. Most of the time you will know what is comfortable with the other person; if not, ask. Another way to establish comfort, particularly when hugging a gal who is not your spouse, is to open your arms and let them determine the hug style. Most ladies will greet the invitation of open arms by responding with what is comfortable for them. They will offer a cheek to brush against or and "A" Frame or they will step forward for a greater degree of closeness including a bear hug. Some will extend a hand for a handshake. Remember, if it isn't natural for them, it is not right. And natural means natural for both parties.

Caressing

The caress needs to be reserved for the significant others. There may be a gray area where friends can share a massaging touch to the knotted muscles of the neck or upper shoulders. But that's all. Caressing is for lovers. As such, it is highly personal and private to the individuals involved.

Dancing

Now we have a live one to tackle. Today's dances look like rejected tribal rituals involving persons having practically nothing to do with each other. Dancing is more in the category of an aerobic demonstration than a touching experience. But wait. To those readers who have matured a bit or watched some old movies, dancing can be a totally different experience.

In early youth, dancing was a cruel and unusual punishment exacted indiscriminately on both sexes. However, as the hormone levels advanced, dancing became a great way to get close to a person and possibly, maybe if you were real lucky, touch. It still can be if you are fortunate enough to find some appropriate music. Of course, there were and probably are exceptions, like the girl in high school who held you off at such a distance that you were sure she also taught stiff-arming to the football team.

TOUCHING DO'S

- Remember that touching relates to tenderness. Squeezes or hugs that are too tight are not good.

- Smile with the touch; in fact, a smile is a visual touch.

- Consider neck massages or back rubs. Most persons need both to combat the tensions of the day.

- If hugging or intending to hug someone you do not know well, ask permission. A good way to do this without being too awkward is to ask, "Have you had your hug today?" If she says, "Yes," and moves away, you have an answer. Most will say, "No," or "I can always use another."

<u>TOUCHING DON'TS</u>

- Force a hug; let it happen.

- Caress in public; it may bother others.

- Concentrate touching in erogenous zones

The Kiss

Ah, the kiss; the tender touching of ones lips to your lover's lips, cheek, nose, forehead, or head. The kiss is one of the most celebrated gestures of all time. It is an unmistaken gesture of love.

It is curious, but often true, that the gentler the kiss the more the love is imparted. The list that follows is just do's. The don'ts are the opposite.

<u>KISSING DO'S</u>

- Kiss gently.

- Kiss more than the lips. Wander a bit.

- Keep the tongue monster behind the lips—reserve that for passion.

- Kiss hurts. All persons are still children at heart (I hope).

Alas, Dear Reader, we have finished "Why," "Who," "How" and "What." All that remains is "When and Where."

PART V
WHEN AND WHERE

12

Occasions

o o o o o o o o o o o o o o o o o o o o o o o o o o o o o o

"If we use no ceremony toward others we shall be treated without any."

—*William Hazlin*

I suppose that even the densest of us know that certain occasions suggest, or more accurately, demand, require and otherwise make it imperative that something be done. Anyone forgetting a birthday or anniversary has learned the hard way. The prudent man will learn early what his love expects and enjoys. For example, Peg loves cards. The absence of a card is significant and affects how she feels. Even with a gift, the card says something not said by the gift. I would suggest to us all that our loves each have a list of expectations, which we need to discover and to which we need to be faithful.

Unfortunately we seldom sit and discuss expectations of this sort. It's almost as if we are supposed to be blessed with special insight. "I just thought you would have known that it is appropriate to exchange potted oak trees on Arbor Day." Since most of us lack this special insight, we must discover these expectations through other means. Some hints are:

• Listen for hints. Most women drop them.

• Ask family, "What do you celebrate?"

- "What did you do for the holidays when growing up?"

- "What did you do with your friends growing up?"

- "Do you celebrate Arbor Day?"

- When you blow it, make a written or mental note or have the lesson tattooed on your thigh. To repeatedly blow it is really very bad form.

A beautiful opportunity between lovers is developing your own occasion, your own occasions. Each couple will have a special time or times in a special place or doing things together which are special. There are no rules, hints or guidelines here. If an occasion, place or activity is romantic to you once, try it again, again, and again.

And now, a word from Americus, Georgia. "I have noted that you like quotations. Why are they all at the beginning of chapters? Can't you put one here?"

Why yes, Americus, How about one from Henry Wadsworth Longfellow?

> *"The holiest of holidays are those kept by ourselves in silence and apart, the secret anniversaries of the heart, when the full tide of feeling overflows."*

Now, before you continue, Americus, please allow the word "ourselves" to refer to a couple rather than all alone. Taken this way makes this quotation a beautiful statement about a very romantic type of occasion.

Also, reflect upon what was said in chapter seven, "Flowers," about non-occasions. Romantic gestures can transform non-occasions into occasions. If you are getting the drift that gestures are appropriate all the time, you are right. Just be sure that the actual occasions of note are noted and observed.

Valentine's Day

Of all the occasions we celebrate, only one is truly an exclusively romantic observance. That's Valentine's Day. Sure, anniversaries are celebrated between just you two, but they are primarily celebrating the history of your relationship. Yes, both are special. It's just that Valentine's Day seems a little more special.

One of the differences is that anniversaries are celebrated by the whole family and may even involve one of those wonderful or terrible things called a surprise party. Valentine's day is more individual, more specific, more personal.

It celebrates "love," not length of time. In that regard, it is current. Your celebration of Valentine's Day this year expresses your love right now. Valentine's Day also carries with it the feeling of youth. Can you walk through a store and see the inexpensive bags of valentines without thinking of how you probably bought a bunch in grade school and anguished or delighted in who got which ones?

So, what do we do for this special time? How should we celebrate? Probably, you begin with the card and maybe a nice gift. Many go with the formal celebration—candy, flowers and dinner out. That's great and far ahead of some who don't do anything.

But think for a moment about once in a while pulling out a few more stops. Think of making it really special. Here is a list of valentine ideas:

Valentine Ideas for Special Celebration

- Buy a balloon instead of, or in addition to, flowers. This year one place was featuring a very large red balloon that was rigged to resemble a hot air balloon with a basket underneath. The basket fits a stuffed animal or candy or whatever.

- Arrange a singing message. Look in the paper. They are advertised. You select the song and can record a personal message.

- Stay home for dinner unless you really can't carry it off properly. If you can, do it and have the table set before she gets home.

- Have the flowers delivered while you are waiting for dinner to get done. (This one is hard because of delivery schedules, but worth a try.)

- Candles are always romantic.

- Music with candles is great.

- Prepare a little speech of love. Don't lead with this. Let the dinner, candles, music, flowers and balloons do the softening, then lay on the love language.

- Consider each Valentine's Day as different and mix up the combinations of the above so that each celebration is special.

Anniversary

Anniversaries are a special form of occasion with wedding anniversaries being at the top. More men get into trouble forgetting a wedding anniversary than any other occasion including a spouse's birthday. (Don't forget the birthday, either.) Please note that each anniversary has a type of gift associated with it. Some try to follow the guide while others couldn't care less. Also note that every 5th year, the anniversaries are more special—every 10th, and even more so, with the 25th and 50th being very special. With population aging as well as it is, add the 75th.

Presents for anniversaries vary widely. Some couples make it a big deal. For others, a special dinner is the prize. If a special project is planned, such as the addition of a sun room, the couple may want to consider this their present to each other. ALERT, ALERT, ALERT. If you ever agree to not exchange presents, strongly consider a card and possibly a small present anyway. When you say, "I couldn't help it. I just had to get this for you," you gain more romantic points (This is not scorekeeping). Over time, you will work this out so that not getting a present is really what is meant all the way to the other extreme of getting significant presents, even when you agree not to. The key is, when in doubt, get. It is easier to apologize for *getting*, than for *forgetting*. Consider this statement: "I thought you would know that not getting anything didn't mean not getting ANYTHING."

Anniversaries are not just commemorations of weddings. Not all get married and some are pre-married. There is no limit to what you can celebrate. One week after first kiss, first year in home or apartment, one month after.... You get the point. Actually, two points. First is that any event is appropriate. This is a great area for the use of your imagination. Think of something special you shared and commemorate it. The second is don't forget the important ones.

Birthdays

What is there to say? This is a special day and merits due celebration. What is due celebration? Whatever is nurturing and meaningful. For some, it's dinner at Pizza Hut. For others, it may be an intimate black tie event with 100 close friends, a small string quartet and rose petals in the fountain.

Luckily birthdays and anniversaries are a bit easier to plan than some other gestures. It is much more comfortable to sit down and ask, "What do you want to do for...." Hopefully, this will do the trick and provide the platform for planning.

But don't stop there. For the romantic, no event is routine. Each one is an opportunity to do something loving, something a little different, something a little special.

Other Occasions

Anniversaries and birthdays tend to be the major romantic days. Mother's Day is next in line. Then comes the major holidays, such as Christmas or Hanukkah, which are religious days, but have opportunities for love and therefore romance.

Beyond these, you are on your own. The potted oak on Arbor Day may have been facetious, but may be real to a few. It may also be a new idea for all of us. Just remember that each person comes to a relationship with a history of traditions or practices they have enjoyed. Find out about these, enjoy them, and create some traditions of your own.

Romance

Much of what is written in this chapter concerns gifts and presents. That is not the focus. There is a separate chapter on that. The essence of this chapter is that celebrating occasions is part of sharing and therefore part of your relationship. While the celebration may not be romantic by itself, it presents a good opportunity for romantic expression.

The other side is that "special" occasions are a great time for romance. The ice is broken from the routine. You are not bound by the rules, expectations or traditions that may accompany a regular occasion. The giving of gifts opens the door for words, for gestures, for little things that may be uncomfortable at other times. As you plan your occasions, review your gestures and go for it.

13

Going Out and Staying In

o o o o o o o o o o o o o o o o o o o o o o o o o o o o o o o
"...take thine ease, eat, drink and be merry."

—*Luke 7:19*

One of the occasions meriting special treatment is going out. It is different from staying in, particularly in romantic potential. Staying in or staying at home is what most folks do most of the time. It is time which is normally spent in some sort of a mutually agreed upon routine. While I'm doing this, you are doing that. Of course, there is ample time and opportunity for romance. Hope you are taking advantage of that. But there is also much time spent on independent activities. In the extreme, a couple can live together and go about their own thing without even talking.

Then comes going out. In some sense, the couple who behaves like ships passing in the night can continue to act with separation equally well at home or going out. In another sense, going out tends to force a closer proximity to each other and a common destination which is conducive, one would think, to a better communication, opportunity for sharing and the like.

In the real sense, the romantic sense, the situation is quite different. Going out is a date. Even if you have been married 52 years, it can still be a date. Of course, that statement does not go unchallenged.

This challenge comes from Chignik Lake, Alaska. "What do you mean dating? When I dated, I was doing all those fun things to get her to like me. Now that we are married, I don't have to do all those things."

Well, thank you, Chignik Lake. You have made my point. But just to make sure, I will restate it. If courtship is a single stage leading to enslavement consummated at the high altar of marriage, we have real problems. If a relationship is really built upon being in love and sharing that love, then courtship is merely the beginning. Romance can continue, if you want it to. It can also die, if you want it to or you let it. The choice is yours. If you wish to keep the romantic spark alive, then what better way is there of looking at going out than considering it a date?

So now that you are going out on a date, what do you do? Well, you do the same things you did when you were on earlier dates. You open doors, use flowers and word gestures and the like. There is a list of hints a bit later. It's not that going out changes who you are or who she is. It's just that this is a special time to have an easy way to be more romantic. Just stuff your head with the phrase, 'this is a date', 'this is a date.' The rest will follow. This may be particularly important to those who have a hard time being romantic. Going out can make it easier.

Another challenge comes from Midnight, Mississippi. Midnight's challenge is, "Oh Author Person, what about going to the grocery? Find something romantic about that."

Well, Midnight, that's easy. You can begin by pushing the cart and saying, "Would you like me to drive?" Next you can go to the flower area, pick a bouquet and say, "I think you should have these." Next stop, candles. Pause and say, "Do we need candles for a candle light dinner?" After this, you look for a cute stuffed animal. There are bound to be some. Slip it into the cart and say nothing. When she discovers it and makes you put it back, you say with your impish smile, "It was cuddly, just like you are." And the list goes on.

Thanks, Midnight, for the grocery store example. There are many of these examples. The important point is that every outing can be a date, can be an occasion for romantic gestures. Just use the *date* mind set.

Hints for Going Out

- Many gas stations have roses for sale at the cashier. Buy one, not every time, just once in a while. Buy it even if you are not going anywhere near a vase. You're expressing thought and feeling. That is the gesture. The rose may wilt, but the thought will remain.

- If you know where you are going, call for a reservation and ask for the most romantic spot. Most establishments, restaurants, hotels, etc. are responsive. Most of the persons working there will enjoy participating in a romantic gesture you have created.

- Expensive, but great, is a bouquet or arrangement on the table in the restaurant or in the hotel room when you arrive.

- A variation of the above is to slip away from the hotel or restaurant and stop at the flower shop in the lobby or around the corner. You, of course, were looking for it all the time. For a really special add on, have the flowers delivered and not brought in by you.

- When driving, take advantage of scenic points. They can be awe-inspiring. Take her hand and say, "I'm glad we can share this."

- When on a long trip, suggest a bit of time down a side road to visit a small town. Pick a town with a unique name, like Peculiar, Missouri, and suggest driving through.

- Don't overload trips or outings. Take the time to enjoy just being together.

- At gift shops, like the ones attached to each tourist attraction, look for something for her. Try buying it without her seeing you and present it 30 miles down the road.

- Ask if she wants to pull over and fool around or whatever your term is for sharing a bit of risqué activity. It is not suggested you do so, but the suggestion is the gesture. If she accepts the offer, you are entirely on your own.

- Suggest a stroll. (That's going out.)

- If you are going out frequently to do the same thing with the same people, suggest a variation. Go alone or do something different.

- When in the car, reach over and hold her hand. For road safety, just give it a squeeze.

- When going between home and a frequent destination, take a different route and express that you are doing so to be romantic.

<u>Staying In</u>

Earlier, it was observed that if you normally stay in, go out. If you normally go out, stay in tonight. The idea was to do something different. As has often been observed, variety is the spice of life, and romantic gestures are the spice of love. Doing something different is a start, but only a start.

Now we hear from Joe Smith of Seattle, Washington. Joe says, "I got the doing something different. I can handle going out because I do what you said and treat it like a date. But what do I do staying in? When we stay in, it's the same thing every night. None of it is romantic."

Thank you Joe. That is a very valid question.

Joe brings up a legitimate concern. Staying in may be doubly difficult because of the routines we all have when we are at home. Many couples, most people, get into a pattern of routines that are well established. This is not bad. Certainly, routines can be good or bad in their own right. Having routines is more desirable than chaos. The point is that the routine is just that, routine. This connotes maybe lack of excitement and exuberation. As with most points, there are exceptions. The key is to appreciate that the romantic side may have competition for time and attention with routine.

The best way to handle this is to agree in advance that something different will be done tonight for the next hour or next few moments or two. Maybe for some, this will be simple. However, some of our group have difficulty in gestures by themselves. Gestures competing with routine can be too much. For these, we return to the basics. A beginning might be, "What would you think of doing something different some night?" he says.

"You mean with a different channel?" she says.

"No, I was thinking of a non TV time," he says.

"Well, we always play bridge every Thursday," she says.

"I was thinking some time at home, with just the two of us," he says.

"Well,…that's sure different."

At this point, there may very well be a slight smile showing on her face. Each script will be different. The important part is to agree to have some time, which is not routine, which is open to some romance or romantic gestures.

The other enemy of staying in time is the schedule, the calendar. You may do nothing routine, but you could be busy almost all the time. Here it might be appropriate for the partners to pencil in time with each other on the calendars. Instead of, "Why don't you have your people get in touch with my people and we will do lunch," you could say, "I'll tell my people I can't be with them, and you and I can stay home all by ourselves." Romance does take some time. If the time is not readily available, some work needs to take place to make some time.

So, now you are together and you have some time. By the way, it does not need to be evening. It can be any time, any day, but some time. How that time is spent is subject to all of the variety one can imagine. If it's romantic, it's loving and nurturing. Let the variety work.

Here is a list of possibilities.

Ideas of What to Do Staying In

- Rent a romantic movie, do popcorn and sit next to each other, not in separate places.

- Talk, just talk. Make plans for a trip, for the future, share feelings, share appreciation of each other.

- Do a special dinner in with candlelight or soft music.

- Take a walk around your yard, the block, the neighborhood. Don't forget to hold hands.

- Bake some bread or cookies for someone else. Share in the making and the giving.

- Go through your scrapbook or photo collection. Share memories.

- Play a board game you haven't done in years. Only do this if you have you competitive spirit under control.

- Have a special dessert, coffee, or tea or whatever. Just make sure it's an occasion.

The list is only a starting point. Think of what you each like to do, and do it together. Don't worry if you don't have the great ideas before you start. Begin by asking to spend more time together, alone. Then chat about what you want to do. If you both draw blanks, pull out this book and look at the list.

PART VI
OTHER STUFF

14

Cautions

"None pities him that is in a snare who warned before would not beware."

—Robert Herrick

"Look before you leap; see before you go."

—Thomas Tusser

It would be great to think that everything that this book is about would be well received, that it would be a positive influence on those who read it and use the ideas. Unfortunately, things can go wrong. There is truth to the adage that the best laid plans of mice and men can go astray. (Don't worry, I don't do mice things. They will need to get their own spokesperson.) However, as regards men, plans don't always work, or work well.

Jackpot, Nevada, pipes up and says, "What can go wrong? It all makes sense and you would think that anyone would know when to do what."

Well, that's all well and good, Jackpot, but totally misses the mark. We don't all know the who, how, what, when and where parts. That's why we have a book. The topic is not natural to all. Also important is the fact that even the most knowledgeable, smoothest, well meaning, discerning man type person can flat out screw up.

So, we need cautions. What are they? The major cautions are:

- One size does not fit all.

- Evolution, not revolution

- Comfort Zone

- Wrong tool for job

- Sincerity is critical

One Size Does Not Fit All

Each of us is a unique individual. Just as fingerprints vary, so do we all have differences in how we like to be treated and romanced. There are individuals out there for whom many gestures in this book will back-fire. This is not a negative observation about those individuals. After all, we are individuals. Actually, it would be pretty dull if we were all the same.

For most of us, romantic gestures work. Some work better than others and some don't work for some individuals. Except for some really difficult cases, all of us have collections of gestures which will express what is important to express and be nurturing in the process. Hard cases have a separate chapter. For the rest of us, some cautions are appropriate.

Maybe some examples are called for. Some women are allergic to flowers or perfumes. By the same token, giving candy to a diabetic is saying the wrong thing. Giving candy to a larger lady can be taken as positive or negative. Another area of caution could be words. Picture a woman who lost a spouse and is very tentative about new romantic relationships. If her new friend uses a pet phrase that her spouse used to use, it may trigger a flood of tears.

Does this mean to be so cautious that you are fearful of doing anything? Certainly not. The idea that is being conveyed is that one size does not fit all. All gestures don't have the same effect or impact. All persons appreciate gestures, but some gestures mean more to one than another. And so on for time, place, and all other aspects of gestures.

Success at any human endeavor takes a bit of risk. We all need to venture forth and try. Even saying "Good morning" to some individuals may result in groping around for your head which has just been bitten off at the neck. Is this the norm? Certainly not. Does this mean that one should not try? I certainly hope not.

The point is to be sensitive to whom and what you are and who and what she is about. As said before, the best test is to ask if the gesture is likely to be nurturing.

Evolution not Revolution

Most romances are the result of nurture and growth over time. They follow our plant example of starting as a seed, being cared for, watered over time. This suggests the evolution of a relationship.

Applying this to gestures would suggest that gestures be tried, some accepted, some rejected, some used frequently, some used very infrequently, new ones tried but not all at once and some saved for that special occasion. Most important is that there be a steady stream of gestures.

The other way to say this is that one should not attack and bombard with gestures as in a revolution. The gentle rain nurtures. The hurricane destroys. Nurture. Nurture. Nurture.

Comfort Zone

The concept of comfort zone shows up in all kinds of subjects. It simply says that there is a zone where we are comfortable and outside of that zone, we are very uncomfortable. Given that, it is wise to stay within or close to your own comfort zone as opposed to going far away from it. The concept includes the thought that you sometimes need to get a bit out of your comfort zone in order to grow. We all need to grow and growth can mean doing some different things outside of our comfort zone in order to expand it a bit.

So what does this have to do with caution? The giver and receiver of a romantic gesture both have a comfort zone. The gesture should fit these comfort zones or come close to them. Again, the nurturing test can come in handy. If the gesture is nurturing, it is probably within the comfort zones.

Also, observe that the reference is to zones, both zones. If the zones are not the same, then discomfort can occur. Most couples share similar comfort zones. But as individuals, their zones may have some parts which are different from the parts they share.

Can't Think of Everything

Sometimes, my friend, a gesture will flat out backfire. I have had one or two classic screw ups. Oh yes, I have made mistakes and so will you. But, I've done a lot right and so will you. Not to try is the pathetic posture.

The point, the real point, is that if we have a foundation of love and romantic gestures, mistakes are forgiven and the screw ups just become part of the stories we tell and share. We need the capacity to admit mistakes and to apologize and go on. This applies to all kinds of situations, all kinds of events and situations.

Wrong Tool for the Wrong Job

Those of us who include fix-it items on our to do list can relate to the frustration of having the wrong tool for the job at hand. Having or using the wrong tool results in not getting the job done or requiring an inordinate amount of time and effort. And so it is with romantic gestures. Gestures vary in impact, intensity, appropriateness, occasion and on and on it goes.

When thinking of a romantic gesture, think through the situation. Not all gestures fit all situations. Not all gestures fit the giver of the gestures, and not all gestures fit the recipient of the gesture.

Sincerity

Of all the factors that can kill the effect of a gesture, lack of sincerity is the deadliest. If we are awkward and sincere, it is okay. In fact, it might even be described as "cute." But lack of sincerity is not.

How do women spot insincerity? There probably is not adequate scientific evidence, but there is plenty of experimental and experiential evidence of the phenomenon. My theory holds that women have a secret chamber in their head. In this secret chamber is a highly sophisticated radar unit. This unit can reach and search another human being in a Nano second and come to conclusions. When women meet other women, it judges, "She's okay. I can share with her," or "That one is not real, a total phony," or "I bet she is out for herself only." It's uncanny and amazingly accurate. Now, this same radar does a number on men. It comes through with, "That's not where you were," or "You spent it on what?" or "I don't believe you." Any man who has embellished a situation (that's a lie), or made up a story (that's a fib), knows that even the best-prepared story is not radar proof. Most men don't have such radar. Oh, maybe a few do, but that is clearly the exception. It is because most of us don't have it that we are so easily caught in the trap of underrating either the existence or the effectiveness of this female radar.

Now that we have established the existence of the radar, we can apply this scientific observation to sincerity. If you are insincere, the radar will nail it. If we are sincere, this same radar will pick it up.

We men love to fool ourselves with our view of our imagined abilities versus our real abilities. Have you ever gone out for a pickup game of football or basketball thinking you were the world's gift to the sport, only to have your body wrench you back into reality with a muscle, tendon or such that forgot for which team it was playing? And how about us golfer types? I play army golf; right, left, right, left from one side of the course to the other. More than I would like, I hit the ball into shrubs or trees rather than into the generous mowed areas of grass. I follow that shot with an attempt to hit a precision shot between two or more trees, with a low trajectory to avoid branches. I have not learned from my experience. I believe, of course, that I can do it.

This same kind of glorious male thinking goes into our attempts to "appear romantic." Forget it. Remember the radar. If you aren't sincere, work on that and what you really feel, not the exquisiteness of the gesture.

The Cautious Conclusion

I don't want to overdo this caution thing, but felt it necessary to raise the point. For the most part, romantic gestures are nothing but positive. When things backfire, apologize and go on. When not sure, nurture, nurture, nurture. When not sure about nurture, nurture, nurture, —ask, ask, ask.

15

Hard Cases

"I don't like these cold, precise, perfect people, who, in order not to speak wrong, never speak at all, and in order not to do wrong, never do anything."

—*Henry Ward Beecher*

"Hope springs eternal in the human breast, man never is, but always to be blest."

—*Alexander Pope*

A hard case is a person who has difficulty with romantic gestures or a situation that does not lend itself to romance. There probably are three types to cover. You are the hard case. Your significant other is the hard case. And finally, the situation is the hard case.

To begin, let's tackle the reader as the hard case (that's you). If you find it hard to picture yourself doing any of the romantic gestures, or you just know you will be embarrassed, or you otherwise detest, abhor or refuse to try any of the suggestions, you are probably a hard case. Are the rest of us giving up on you? No Way! Try this quiz. Did you look at the table of contents, find the chapter on Hard Cases and turn immediately to this page? If so, you possess a major qualification for being a hard case. On the other hand, if you read up to this point, then you are curious, intrigued and have a fair interest in the subject. To be blunt, the real hard cases would never open this book. Everyone who has exhibits some interest and curiosity about romance. That is all that is necessary.

If you think you are a hard case, regardless of degree, there is hope and hope springs eternal…. Begin your journey with the single step. Pick out of this book the one idea or thought, which is least bothersome to you and try it. Just one, a simple one. If it does work, try again. If it doesn't work, consider this question to your significant other, "Hey, (Insert your pet name, hopefully something nice), I'm having just a bit of trouble here. I did so and so to be nice and it is not working. What's wrong?"

Be prepared for a variety of answers from, "Oh, I'm sorry. I didn't know it was for me," or "You dumb oaf, pick the dandelions before you mow, not after!" to "I didn't know what you were doing." If you get a response, "I don't want any of your stupid stuff," then you may have a hard case on the other side.

If your heart is right and you pick a gesture that is consistent with who, what, when and where, you are and who, what, when and where your partner is, chances for success are fairly high. You can always show your copy of the book and ask, "Can we look at this together?" If something backfires, just blame me and this*!#@%*book.

Some Hints for Hard Cases

- A single flower

- A Thank You

- A small compliment

- A hug

- A pat on the hand

- A smile

- A card

The next situation is Ms. Hard Case. Are there women who avoid romantic gestures? Probably, but hopefully few. If you try a simple gesture or two and are burned from the backfire, try this review.

Hard Case Review

- Was my gesture simple enough?

- Was my gesture nurturing?

- Would another gesture have worked better?

- Does my friend have things that are bothering her so that the gesture is overshadowed?

- Was the occasion proper?

- Was the timing proper?

- Did I do it okay, flub it?

- Was her reaction for the gesture or for me or for something else?

This list, as the others, could go on and on. The point is that you must be sensitive to your significant other. If you are sensitive to your significant other and honest in your review, you should come up with a clue as to whether this seems to be a hard case on her part or yours. The situation is the same whether you or your lady is the hard case. If this is happening, try again. Sit and talk or consider that there may be some real problems between you.

The final point on hard cases is the situation. The word situation is being used in the broadest sense. Situations can be the who, what, why, when and where of the gesture or attempted gesture. Some of us men type creatures are just clumsy when it comes to this stuff. Our hearts can be as pure as gold but we can come off as a complete oaf. If this is your tendency, don't give up. Stay sensitive and keep going for simplicity. Maybe the purest gesture is the statement, "I'm trying to be more romantic but it's not going well. Can you help me?" If done honestly and sincerely, it should open any door that is going to open. No guarantees but hang in there and best of everything.

16

Sex

"The sexes were made for each other, and only in the wise and loving union of the two is the fullness of health and duty and happiness to be expected."

—*William Hall*

The sexual intimacy shared by two persons can be the most beautiful time imaginable.... It can also be ugly. What is the difference? Much has to do with whether the event is love, which includes passion, or is an event of passion by itself. We are concerned with romance and love. How to improve your sex life is a totally different topic and discussed elsewhere. The premise of this chapter is that the romantic process includes the intimacy of sex. Being loving can lead to sex. Having sex does not mean that love results.

The place for romance in sex is the caring, sharing and nurturing, which is normally expressed but may be more intense surrounding the act of passion. It is touching, the words, the expressions before and after. It is setting the stage in which the act of union is a natural extension of the romance.

There is one other area which merits discussion. That is intimacy. There is a great misconception that sex is intimacy and intimacy is sex. There is a relationship in that sex is <u>an</u> intimacy. But intimacy is far more. Intimacy is opening yourself to another. It is sharing and communicating what is going on inside your head, heart and spirit. Intimacy is saying here is where I hurt, here is where I have joy, here is where I am afraid, here is where I love. An interesting way to look at intimacy was expressed at a conference I once attended as IN TO ME SEE. Most intimacy has nothing to do with sex. But sexual intimacy is enhanced when real intimacy exists.

This is another chapter that merits some do's and don'ts, so here they are.

Do List for the Romantic Side of Sex

- Do plan to take your lover away occasionally to a romantic spot.

- Do return to your honeymoon spot.

- Do understand that the orgasms experienced by men and women are very different. Women like to continue to be held and loved after the climax.

- Do express appreciation of the person, not just the body.

- Do take time. Let passion build.

- Do include a lot of holding and touching.

- Do discuss what you each enjoy.

- Do express your appreciation for spending time and sharing each other.

- Do think of other gestures on occasions of passion. For example, flowers and, of course, words.

- Do remember sex is sharing. It is not a right, obligation or duty.

- Do try to be spontaneous. Try different things, different times.

Don't List of the Romantic Side of Sex

- Don't think of your satisfaction only. This is a time for sharing like no other.

- Don't look at the union as an end, but part of a relationship.

- Don't forget to take care of your own body. Unless it is specifically a turn on for your partner, shave and bathe. Most women do not find it sexy to be sand papered by a beard or have a smell like you just spent a week doing hard labor.

- Don't turn on the TV right after love, or during.

- Don't assume that owning a penis creates an understanding of what your partner wants. Discuss what is enjoyed.

- Don't abruptly leave after you have done your thing. Linger.

- Don't do the same things all the time. This produces routine and routine can be deadly.

- Don't get stuck in "every Saturday night," unless that is really what both want.

17

Curable or Not

o o o o o o o o o o o o o o o o o o o o o o o o o o o o o o o
"Why do I want to be cured when I enjoy my condition."

—*Overheard in a waiting room*

It is indeed unfortunate that there is even the thought of being a cured romantic. This world is rampant with violence, abuse, sarcasm and distrust. The world desperately needs more of what is embodied in romantic behavior. Who can argue that nurturing is wrong or bad? Who can argue against gentleness, mildness? Who can possible argue against the expression of love?

No, my friend, we need romantics. We need them personally. We need them societally. We need more positive and less negative. I pray to God that I am never cured and hope you join in that thought.

18

Technology

"When men are easy in their circumstances, they are natural enemies to innovation."

—*Joseph Addison*

Man, did that title draw the phone calls. The best two were from Key Largo, Florida, and Ticonderoga, New York. They essentially said the same thing. "Why in the #@C:/.@+have you put in something about technology when everywhere else you are ranting and raving about direct people to people romantic things?"

Slow down callers; ranting and raving is a bit strong. I am not suggesting that technology take the place of holding hands, but to ignore the impact of technology on today and tomorrow's world is unwise, if not irresponsible.

We need to put some perspective on the word technology. Think of technology as a set of tools and not an end in itself. Technology is certainly part of how we communicate. That communication can be romantic as well as anything else. As more and more individuals spend more time on their PC's and the Internet, it is important to understand how romantic gestures may fit. My comments are not, repeat *not*, covering the X-rated chat rooms and other marginal practices. As with any human enterprise, E-mail and the online or Internet environment will draw abusive use as well as constructive.

Desk Top Publishing

This is a great place to start since just about everyone has some word processing software. In the formal sense, desktop publishing refers to an advanced use of the word processing tools to create materials that can go right to the printing company from the PC. In a more practical sense, any letter, memo or other output from any word processing program is a publication from your desktop computer. So whether you are doing Ventura or just using Word or Word Perfect, you have opportunities for publications.

To start, consider designing your own greeting card. The down side is that your lady could consider that cheap. The up side is that you cared enough to do it personally. This is a great opportunity to fashion the words to just what you want. I don't know about you, but I have often been frustrated in picking out a card when the picture is perfect but the text just doesn't fit. Make up your own, quote from a poem or borrow the phrase from a store bought card and put it in your own creation. Of course, there are the problems of copyright law, so maybe you should just look for ideas, not actual text. I certainly don't want to get hauled into court as an accomplice in a $10,000,000 lawsuit where a card company sues a chap for saying, "I love you."

Next is the graphics side. All word processing has a bit of clip art which can be imported and placed into or all over your creation. If you don't have enough, you can always buy 5,000 to 15,000 additional images at a low cost.

The result may not be professional, but the idea that you cared and did something with your little mouse is important. Have you ever seen a refrigerator with art from a 5, 6, 7 or 8 year old? Not normally impressive…but appreciated? You got it.

Lest we lose balance, it may be that you use homemade to spice up life along with purchased cards. I also don't want to get sued by Hallmark, a local company to me, for ruining the card business. There are also cards you can design at card stores using manufacturer's own software and machines.

Don't stop yet. Cards are only one dimension. Consider notes requesting a date. You know, let's stay in or let's go out. Consider the previously mentioned certificates good for one night of doing dishes or one free washing of her car—by your own little hands. How about a gift certificate good for a weekend getaway at a special place. Use your own imagination. Try creating a menu of what you are serving for a special dinner.

You can also spice up a note or letter by adding a heart or a flower from the clip art. Just think romantically as you stroke your keyboard and meander your mouse.

E-mail

More and more communication is going by e-mail. If you and your significant other have e-mail, you will undoubtedly use it for some of your communications.

Please keep in mind that most e-mail is not as secure as you would like. Just imagine that you are on a party line. Save the real juicy stuff for when you are in person.

E-mail is not very romantic by itself. One of the things you can do is add some character art. A few examples are:

Hugs and Kisses   [] :*

Happy Faces   :-)

If you want more. just ask your local neighborhood tecky and you will get more than you need. Another source is on the internet. Just search using the term "smiley." If you don't see the picture, turn the page sideways. The colons are the eyes.

Internet

The internet is still in infancy at this writing. Certainly the growth is explosive. But whether the mature internet is the communication end all and be all is yet to be determined.

But you can buy flowers, shop for event tickets, printout great art for your creations, send e-mail and even spend an evening together surfing.

While it is not clear how the internet will play a role in romance, it is clear that surfing can be addictive and can interfere with romance. It is also clear that some persons use chat rooms and bulletin boards for their social life. We have some interesting challenges in how we use technology. Maybe it is time to repeat—balance, balance, balance.

19

Advanced Topics

○ ○
"Not to go back is somewhat advanced. And men must walk at least before they dance."

—*Alexander Pope*

Until this chapter, I have been cautious about pouring on too much at once. I have cautioned to go slow, try things, experiment, but don't go overboard. "I cant's" define overboard in any absolute sense. Overboard is just something that is too much for that person, at that time, or that gesture or presented that way. Very, very individualistic and personal.

There are times when you need to or want to do something more advanced, unique or maybe overboard. This could come out of a relationship that is well established and already full of many of the gestures that have been presented. It could come out of a heart that is absolutely bursting with love and needing some special expression. And it could come out of a need to for this time, for that person, go overboard.

For whatever reasons you may have need of a hint for an advanced gesture. A good place to start is a review of the ideas under unique gifts. The distinction between unique and advanced is blurred at best. After you have skimmed that section, return here and proceed.

Write a Poem

Poetry is the language of love. Poetry is sometimes linked to expressing the matters of the spirit, the heart, the inner person. It is a special form of writing which evokes a special response.

Not everyone likes poetry. And not everyone can write poetry. If it doesn't fit, don't try it. However, if she likes it and you can do it, then have at it. This is a great point for reader challenge, and there is one. From Incline Village, Nevada, comes the challenge of: "What, Dear Author Friend, do I do if I want the poem, but don't have any poetic bones in my pathetic body?"

Not to fear Incline, there are ways.

There are two ready sources of help. One is the library which will have much on how to write poetry. The next area of help is your local card store. Go in and read all the cards of a romantic nature. Out of the collection should come many ideas, lines of poetry or phrases or even word rhyming which may be helpful. So, friend, dedicate a portion of a tree and a bit of your time to taking a stab at poetry. Remember, however, that even the world's worst poem is still a romantic gesture and will most likely be better received than the composer, excuse me, poet, feels it will be.

For some, including our associate from Incline who doesn't have a poetic bone in his body, another approach may be necessary. The simplest alternative is to buy the book of poetry or the card with the right poem. You can always say, "Sweetheart, I got this for you because I can't write poetry. But if I could write poetry, I would have written something just like this." That should work. Want it more personal? Copy the poem in your own hand with a short statement like the one above. Finally, you can get a friend or even a distant acquaintance who does poetry to write for you. You can tell them what you want and go from there. Don't claim you wrote it, if you didn't. Just say, "I had this written for you," or if you paid for it, "I commissioned this poem just for you."

Commissioning a Piece of Art

Don't worry; I'm not suggesting a $50,000 extravaganza. Although, If you have big bucks, that would work. What I am suggesting is the uniqueness of a commissioned piece. Everyone can buy gifts, art included. But to commission a piece means that it is truly unique and special. And, let's face it, the term 'commissioned' sounds like a big ticket.

Now, as to what to commission. How about a new building for the museum in town? (Just kidding.) Begin with ceramics or pottery. This could be a dish or bowl or just an art piece. Continuing along the craft trail could be some clothing, woodworking or leather. All you need to do is go to a craft show and walk around for ideas. If you see something that might work, ask the person if they do commission work. This assumes that nothing they have out will work or work well. If you spot the perfect item, get it. Commissioning is where you want that special, unique piece that you just can't find already done.

Also, in the craft/art area is stained glass. This is a great idea for commissioning. Most do not have a great deal of stained glass. This means that an additional piece will stand out. It is also an excellent area for personalized uniqueness. For example, if your lady loves likes daffodils, then your stained glass of daffodils is a year round exhibit of her favorite flower. She could love angels, peaceful streams or water, covered bridges, etc. In addition to topic, a commission allows you to pick up your favorite colors and moods. Talk to the artist. Discuss what she likes and doesn't like.

Finally, we come to painting and sculpture. These tend to be pricier than stained glass because of the time involved. As with crafts, go to an art fair and shop. If you find the right thing, buy it. If you find an almost right thing, commission getting it the way you really want it.

I'm sure other art forms are listable. Furniture and photographs come to mind and there are others. Don't forget that you are also helping to support the arts even though the commission may be small.

Create Some Music

If a poem is very good, a song could be great. In a song you have both the poetry of the words plus the beauty of the music. Don't try a symphony unless you are really talented, trained and have a lot of time. Remember, the thought is what counts the most. "You wrote a song for me? My own song?"

As with the poem, you can borrow ideas and pieces here and there. You can use your library, sound and video store. You can also get a ghost composer here as well. As with all creative material, be sure you observe the difference between being inspired by another's work and taking it outright.

Serenade

How about performing your new work in person? Not on your life you say? Well, no problem. If there are talents available for artistic commissions to paint, sculpt, write and otherwise create, there are also many who perform and would love some work.

Now that you have brought this up, why not serenade just for fun? It doesn't have to feature your own work. It can just be a serenade. Hire a band or a choir. Too much? What about the men who play at the romantic restaurant you go to; the violinist alone, accordion, if you prefer, or the singer?

It helps if you have a balcony and it's great weather. If not, stage a time at home or somewhere out where you will have the right setting, a lot of people or just you two, and the right feeling, not rushed. Set it up and add a dinner or flowers, or both. You get the idea.

Write a Love Story

So you want to write, but your poems don't rhyme and your music, well, maybe it will never work. What about a love story? It can be your love story. It can have the characters saying things to each other as you would like to say and hear for real.

So, consider. Remember, your loved one is impressed with your effort and thoughtfulness more than the product. She will treasure the special touch of having your hand involved.

The Biplane Billboard

I'm sure you have all seen an occasional billboard saying, "Sue, will you marry me? Ted." The same message can sometimes be found trailing behind a relic biplane over the football stadium. That public type of display is not for all. But for some, with the right message…. You've got to admit that it's an advanced gesture.

Dinner for Two

This doesn't sound advanced, but can be. Let's say you have a rather routine style of eating at the kitchen table. Maybe you also frequently have the TV playing. This is fine and can be a bit romantic. However…

Now picture that your sweetheart also works or does garden club or whatever gets you the house to yourself for the afternoon or day. Sometimes this window of opportunity is when her office holiday schedule is different from yours. If none of that works, conspire with one of her girl friends to get her out for the afternoon.

Begin by shopping for the special meal. Add to that flowers for the table, candles and wine. First, set the table. Use the good china and silver. Set two places. Chill the wine, arrange the flowers and candles. If you have a bunch of candleholders, you may want to set out all or most. A grouping can be great, but don't overdo. Next, start preparing food. Shrimp cocktail is great and easy. Cook the shrimp with a boiling pot of water and lemon juice next to it. You won't smell shrimp in the air after. Many stores cook shrimp for you. Prepare and set plates in the refrigerator to stay cold. Make the salad in advance and refrigerate. Then prepare whatever else you want.

An hour before she comes home, change into a nice outfit. All right, if you have a tux you can wear it. Whatever is appropriate. A half-hour before she's due home, or even 15 minutes, depending on how punctual she is or how reliable the schedule, shift into high gear. Set out the salads, shrimp cocktail or whatever, fill the water glasses, pour the wine and light the candles and put on some soft music.

When she arrives, you show her to her seat, asking if she would like to change or freshen up. Don't rush. Allow her time to digest the surprise and to decompress from whatever she has been doing. Leisurely present the meal, dessert and coffee or tea. If you wish more, present a gift or card. Should you really want to go all out, hire a waiter, a violinist. Why not? Hey, if it's romantic and you can afford, go for it. Chances are she would prefer to be alone with you.

The most successful use of an advanced topic is where it fits the persons involved. If it doesn't fit, it becomes grandstanding. If your style is quiet, the gesture, even advanced, should be quiet. If you are demonstrative, your special gesture may also be demonstrative or may really be special by being quiet.

PART VII

ONE FOR THE GIPPER

20

Give It a Try

"Things don't turn up in this world until someone turns them up."

—*James A. Garfield*

Well, here we are at the end of this book. Now what? Find anything of use? Can you do more than you used to be doing? Remember that the idea is not to do it all, but increase what you are doing.

Need to start slow? OK. Everyone will have his own pace. Recall that no one is keeping score.

Already doing it all? Congratulations. Have some gestures of your own. Great. In fact, I'd love to hear from you.

We all are in different places. That's normal. Most want to enjoy more romance or the result of being more romantic. Most will see what they want to do and are already started.

But there may still be a few. There may still be the skeptic type saying, "I don't think it will work...."

Give it a try.

PART VIII

SUMMARY OF
GUIDES AND LISTS

SUMMARY

✦

Guides and Lists

o o o o o o o o o o o o o o o o o o o o o o o o o o o o o o o o

"A sound head, an honest heart and a humble spirit are the three best guides through time and eternity. That man may safely venture on his way who is so guided that he cannot stray."

—*Walter Scott*

This is the day of add water, stir and serve. Based on this phenomenon, the various guides and lists created in the book are repeated here as a reference. So, the next time you are at a loss for an appropriate gesture and time is running out, dive into this section and go for it.

As mentioned at the end of chapter seven, the list was never to be completed because the list was endless. The real objective of all of these guides and lists is to provide a start and increase sensitivity. Anyone becoming sensitive or increasing sensitivity will do well with the specifics, from these lists or on their own.

From Chapter 2/Foundation Relationships, Page

Phrases for Friends

- Let's just stay here tonight.

- Let's just go out tonight.

- How about a walk?

- How was your day?

- What would you like to do that we haven't done?

- Can I help you with something?

- Are you as happy as you could be...?

- What can I do to make your life more enjoyable?

- I enjoy spending time with you.

- You look sad. Anything I can do?

Chapter 3/Where to Begin, Page

Beginners Questions

- Am I sensitive to our relationship?

- Does the gesture fit the situation?

- Is the gesture nurturing?

- Is this a simple step?

- Was I sincere in my feelings?

- How was it received?

- What is next?

- Did she like that I did something but not like that particular thing?

- Was it the right or wrong time?

- Did I feel good?

Chapter 5/Hint Gathering, Page

Hint Phrases

- I have always wanted…

- I am looking for…

- That is just what I wanted, but I can't afford it right now…

- You know the sweater that Carol was wearing, I would look great in it but in blue…

- George did the nicest thing for Gracie…

- I shouldn't get this should I…?

- What would you think about…?

- Why don't we ever…?

- You will never guess what I saw….

Chapter 5/Hint Gathering, Page

Signals

- She says: "Isn't that the cutest outfit, I'd really love to have one like that."
  She means: "Birthday next month. If I'm getting clothes, that is a great idea."

- She says: "…and they went to that new restaurant, The Plentiful Pig, and just had the greatest time."
  She means: "Why don't we go there soon."

- She says: "….

Chapter 6/The Little Things, Page

The Little Things

- Suggest staying home "just the two of you." You don't even need plans, just time together because you want to be together. Women love relationships. They love to feel wanted, not just in bed or behind the sink or as another paycheck in the home. They want to feel that you truly enjoy their company.

- Suggest going out. You may be observing that this point suggests the opposite of the above. The key is that you suggest something you don't normally do. Go out if the two of you are normally in and stay in if you are normally out. The message is that you wish to be with her. The difference in setting enhances that. Most important is that you are suggesting doing either with her.

- Comment on her hair, wardrobe.

- Pick and present a flower while walking. Giving a flower says, "I love you." It is a great way for those who get tongue tied to make a statement. Be careful not to violate park, state or federal laws. And be cautious not to pick an ugly weed or present a potential sneezing attack to an allergy sufferer.

- Send a card for no reason. Cards vary from full, detailed and elaborate messages to a very simple "thinking of you." Send a card from a business trip location. Pen in the card, "This meeting would be better if you were here." Send a card from the same town. Don't overdo or she will wonder what you are trying to hide.

- Take her hand. Hold it for a while or just give it a squeeze.

- If you have stuffed animals around the house, put one between the blanket and the pillow on her side. If you don't have one get one. If she says, "That's a childish thing to do," respond, "You bring out the kid in me."

- Cook dinner, unless you are a walking culinary crisis.

- Open doors for all women. This costs so little and means so much. Your significant other will appreciate your opening the door for other women. She can say to herself, "See other female person, MY man is courteous." Whether that phrase is followed by the thought, "Eat your heart out," depends upon the individual. One caution is not to overdo. If you stay at the door while waiting for a lady to travel 15 more yards, your lady begins to wonder if you are more concerned with the other one than with her. Another caution is not to expect all women to respond the same way. Some will respond to your courteous action with a warm smile and will say, "Thank you." Others will completely ignore you and your actions. It is recommended that you resist the temptation to shout after them, "You're welcome," oozing sarcasm from every pore.

- If you go to work first, bring in the paper.

- Suggest talking. "Let's just talk instead of watching TV during dinner." This item should not be attempted if you have trouble talking. See the section on Comfort Zone in Chapter Fourteen. However, if talking with each other is comfortable, then suggesting it occasionally is a great move. Women love to talk and to be listened to. John Grey in "Men are from Mars and Women are from Venus" does a great treatment of conversation. Grey makes the point that talking out things is a part of a woman's process of sharing feelings. Be sure that you understand that this implies your role is to listen. Listen, not responding to each point or discuss or debate. Listen, Listen, Listen. If you can read the first few chapters of Grey's book, it is a real insight.

- Offer to do the dishes.

- Offer to do anything that she normally does and you normally don't do. You can say, "Here, let me do that. You always do that, I can take a turn."

- Do the dishes you have offered to do.

- Bring up a cup of tea or coffee while she is still in bed. This is a great one because it is highly appreciated, but does not commit to a full breakfast in bed. Some don't like to have breakfast in bed. Even if some do, there are many things that can go wrong. Everyone has a different routine. The routine may call for much to be done before even "thinking" about food. Others have very specific breakfast ideas. For example, a petite lady may only want tea and a piece of dry toast. To regale her with an omelet and hash browns smothered in country gravy will back fire…. Stay simple, the little things. By the way, a flower on a tray or resting on the saucer is great.

- Dry the dishes you have done.

- Put away the dishes you have dried.

- Hang up the towel you used to dry the dishes.

Chapter 7/Flowers, Page

Flower—Non-Occasions

- Tomorrow is Tuesday.

- Returning from a trip.

- Just because…

- Beginning of spring—The first of May was celebrated with the giving of a May basket containing flowers, but not currently practiced. Maybe the mention here will revive the practice.

- Upon finishing a project or activity.

- Reaching a milestone. Pay off the mortgage—getting you first home, or the first brand new car.

- Getting a raise.

- And on and on.

Chapter 7/Flowers, Page

<u>Flower Do's</u>

- Do ask florists for ideas, particularly if you don't have the feel.

- Do buy fresh flowers.

- Do ask for water pics. This is a little glass vial at the end of a stem, which will prolong the life of the flowers. Particularly ask for this if it will be several hours between purchase and presenting.

- Do check out fashions of the day before getting a corsage. Some ladies hate pin-ons, others hate wrist corsages, and many don't like corsages at all. *Best Bet*: ask a close friend of your lady what her preferences are and what color she will be wearing. When you ask, start with, "Would it be a good idea to…." If you start with, "I'm going to get Brunhilda a corsage…", you are not as open to the response that she may not like a corsage. Remember, her close friend may not want to hurt your feelings, so how you ask is important.

- Do cut off stems an inch or two from the bottom whenever stems have been out of water for a while. The bottom will dry and prevent water from traveling to the blossom. This will make a difference in the life of the flower. A rose, which does not open and just leans over the stem, typically does this because the stem is not carrying water. Incidentally, if you sense that this is happening, immerse the whole flower in water for 25 minutes. This may revive it. When cutting, cut under water, then immediately place in water.

- Do have a vase that fits the flowers. Use a narrow one for a single stem, a broad one for a bunch, etc. As elsewhere, the flowers and the vase should be in balance.

- Do use the plant food package often obtained with fresh flowers. If this is not available, put a bit of sugar in the water. Use warm water in the vase.

- Do ask for a few babies' breath to be part of your bouquet, particularly with roses, whether single or a bouquet. It may cost a bit more, but probably not much.

- Do keep in mind that different flowers may send different messages:

Lilies		Funeral
Roses		
	Red	Love
	White	Purity
	Yellow	Friendship
	Pink	Sweetheart

- Do listen for clues from your loved one. "Aren't those beautiful *so and so's*. I just love *so and so's*.

- Do send flowers by phone. You can now send flowers by calling 24 hours a day and using your plastic. The service charges are very nominal and the results are surprisingly good.

Chapter 7/Flowers, Page

Flower Don'ts

- Don't always give flowers to say you are sorry and then expect them to all of a sudden have a romantic impact.

- Don't give silk flowers as a romantic gesture. They are great as a gift and nice to have, but not very romantic.

- Roses are particularly subject to bargains. A dozen roses for $5.00 is highly suspect. They may last 24 hours and never open. Consider a single quality rose which will slowly open and last for a week or more. The beauty of a quality single rose has much greater impact than almost anything else.

- Don't give the same thing every time. Part of the flower ceremony is surprise. Of course, there is an exception where the relationship is mature and the same thing is a tradition.

- Don't overdo. Gestures that happen too often become habit and lose the edge of impact that a surprise has.

Chapter 8/Words, Page

Affection Statements

- Hi, cutie.

- You look good in that.

- I feel good being with you.

- Buckle up! I don't want anything to happen to you.

- I love it when I'm near you.

- You are the prettiest at this party. No question.

- I love the way your nose turns up.

- If you wear that perfume again, I will not be responsible for my actions. (Hints at passion, but still affectionate.)

- You hands are so soft.

Chapter 8/Words, Page

Appreciation Statements

- Thank you.

- I like it when you…

- You look nice tonight.

- I like that dress.

- Thanks for fixing that dish for dinner.

- I love you.

- I'm glad that I married you.

- You are fun to be with.

- I like spending time with you.

- I appreciate you.

- Twenty years of marriage and you are still my girlfriend.

- I love you, but you are also my best friend.

- That's a great idea.

Chapter 8/Words, Page

Adoration Statements

- I truly love you.

- I cannot imagine life without you.

- You are very precious to me.

- You make life worthwhile.

- I cherish you.

- I adore you.

Chapter 8/Words, Page

Apology Statements

- I'm sorry.

- I misjudged that, I'm sorry.

- I goofed.

- I blew it.

- I screwed up.

- I made a mistake when I...

- I didn't mean to, but I did.

Chapter 8/Words, Page

Affirming Statements

- I'm glad you are here.

- You do...well.

- I don't know how you do it, but....

- I don't know what I would do without you.

- We couldn't be where we are without your special touch.

- You are a treasure.

- I would be nothing without you.

- You are very important in my life.

Chapter 9/Chivalry, Page

CHIVALRY DO'S

- Open car doors. (I heard of one couple having a spat. The lady went to the car and waited to have the door opened for her. The "gentleman," who was angry and preoccupied, went to his side, opened his door, got in, started the car and drove off, assuming his partner had gotten in by herself. This did not cool things off.)

- Allow women to go first. Exception, revolving doors. When approaching the door the man should go first to supply the power. If you are not sure, then say, "Let me get this started." Another exception is the elevator. If you are one of the last on, and it's a relatively full car, get off first and out of the way rather than force her and others to maneuver around you.

- When something is dropped, say, "Let me," and then pick it up. Not to say, "Let me," may invite the knocking of heads as both go after the treasure.

- Ask if you are unsure, "May I open the door?" This will give you immediate feedback.

- Offer to help with packages, luggage.

- Let the lady order first.

Chapter 9/Chivalry, Page

CHIVALRY DON'TS

- Don't object to a lady picking up a tab. It is now fashionable to share. Equality tempers chivalry.

- Don't start eating until all are served. Exception, waiting for a special order or a large group to be served. Ask, "May we go ahead," or wait until someone says, "Please, go ahead."

- Don't start eating until the hostess has begun or until another lady has begun, or either has placed the appropriate piece of silver on the plate. (For more, see a handbook on etiquette, which is heavily connected to chivalry.)

- Don't use bodily functions or sounds as a source of humor. I don't like it even with just the men. I sense that most men laugh only to avoid offending the person sticking out their finger to be pulled.

- Don't verbally put down your partner, even if others are doing it. For that matter, don't put anyone down.

Chapter 10/Gifts and Presents, Page

GIFTS AND PRESENTS DO'S

- Do make gifts personal, nurturing and loving whenever possible.

- Do give gifts at non-occasion times. In other words, make you own occasions.

- Do be sensitive to what she likes, her sizes, what styles she favors, what store she enjoys.

- Do be sensitive to cards.

- Do think of time as a gift.

- Do keep receipts

- Do splurge occasionally for professional gift-wrapping.

- Do be sensitive to when and how a gift is presented.

Chapter 10/Gifts and Presents, Page

GIFTS AND PRESENTS DON'TS

- Don't buy appliances as a romantic gift.

- Don't buy from a store that has a bad return policy.

- Don't toss receipts.

- Don't leave the price tag on the gift.

- Don't give the same thing all the time.

Chapter 10/Gifts and Presents, Page

Coupon Gifts from You

- One night of doing the dishes

- One visit to your mother's without...

- A dinner for two at home. I'll cook.

- A night at that Bed and Breakfast we saw at the lake.

- One day of painting the hallway

- Digging up the old garden plot

- An evening of dancing—I'll even dance.

- Your choice of opera or ballet—I won't yawn.

- Next movie is your choice

- I'll take a day off to help spring clean

- Weekend at any romantic place within 200 miles

- A dinner at the Ritz

- Two hours in the park

- A month of hanging up my clothes

Chapter 11/Touching, Page

TOUCHING DO'S

- Remember that touching relates to tenderness. Squeezes or hugs that are too tight are not good.

- Smile with the touch; in fact, a smile is a visual touch.

- Consider neck massages or back rubs. Most persons need both to combat the tensions of the day.

- If hugging or intending to hug someone you do not know well, ask permission. A good way to do this without being too awkward is to ask, "Have you had your hug today?" If she says, "Yes," and moves away, you have an answer. Most will say, "No," or "I can always use another."

Chapter 11/Touching, Page

TOUCHING DON'TS

- Force a hug; let it happen.

- Caress in public; it may bother others.

- Concentrate touching in erogenous zones

Chapter 11/Touching, Page

KISSING DO'S

- Kiss gently.

- Kiss more than the lips. Wander a bit.

- Keep the tongue monster behind the lips—reserve that for passion.

- Kiss hurts. All persons are still children at heart (I hope).

Chapter 12/Occasions, Page

Occasion Hints

- Listen for hints. Most women drop them.

- Ask family, "What do you celebrate?"

- "What did you do for the holidays when growing up?"

- "What did you do with your friends growing up?"

- "Do you celebrate Arbor Day?"

- When you blow it, make a written or mental note or have the lesson tattooed on your thigh. To repeatedly blow it is really very bad form.

Chapter 12/Occasion, Page

Valentine Ideas for Special Celebration

- Buy a balloon instead of, or in addition to, flowers. This year one place was featuring a very large red balloon that was rigged to resemble a hot air balloon with a basket underneath. The basket fits a stuffed animal or candy or whatever.

- Arrange a singing message. Look in the paper. They are advertised. You select the song and can record a personal message.

- Stay home for dinner unless you really can't carry it off properly. If you can, do it and have the table set before she gets home.

- Have the flowers delivered while you are waiting for dinner to get done. (This one is hard because of delivery schedules, but worth a try.)

- Candles are always romantic.

- Music with candles is great.

- Prepare a little speech of love. Don't lead with this. Let the dinner, candles, music, flowers and balloons do the softening, then lay on the love language.

- Consider each Valentine's Day as different and mix up the combinations of the above so that each celebration is special.

Chapter 13/Going Out, Page

Hints for Going Out

- Many gas stations have roses for sale at the cashier. Buy one, not every time, just once in a while. Buy it even if you are not going anywhere near a vase. You're expressing thought and feeling. That is the gesture. The rose may wilt, but the thought will remain.

- If you know where you are going, call for a reservation and ask for the most romantic spot. Most establishments, restaurants, hotels, etc. are responsive. Most of the persons working there will enjoy participating in a romantic gesture you have created.

- Expensive, but great, is a bouquet or arrangement on the table in the restaurant or in the hotel room when you arrive.

- A variation of the above is to slip away from the hotel or restaurant and stop at the flower shop in the lobby or around the corner. You, of course, were looking for it all the time. For a really special add on, have the flowers delivered and not brought in by you.

- When driving, take advantage of scenic points. They can be awe-inspiring. Take her hand and say, "I'm glad we can share this."

- When on a long trip, suggest a bit of time down a side road to visit a small town. Pick a town with a unique name, like Peculiar, Missouri, and suggest driving through.

- Don't overload trips or outings. Take the time to enjoy just being together.

- At gift shops, like the ones attached to each tourist attraction, look for something for her. Try buying it without her seeing you and present it 30 miles down the road.

- Ask if she wants to pull over and fool around or whatever your term is for sharing a bit of risqué activity. It is not suggested you do so, but the suggestion is the gesture. If she accepts the offer, you are entirely on your own.

- Suggest a stroll. (That's going out.)

- If you are going out frequently to do the same thing with the same people, suggest a variation. Go alone or do something different.

- When in the car, reach over and hold her hand. For road safety, just give it a squeeze.

- When going between home and a frequent destination, take a different route and express that you are doing so to be romantic.

Chapter 13/Going Out, Page

Ideas of What to Do Staying In

- Rent a romantic movie, do popcorn and sit next to each other, not in separate places.

- Talk, just talk. Make plans for a trip, for the future, share feelings, share appreciation of each other.

- Do a special dinner in with candlelight or soft music.

- Take a walk around your yard, the block, the neighborhood. Don't forget to hold hands.

- Bake some bread or cookies for someone else. Share in the making and the giving.

- Go through your scrapbook or photo collection. Share memories.

- Play a board game you haven't done in years. Only do this if you have you competitive spirit under control.

- Have a special dessert, coffee, or tea. Just make sure it's an occasion.

Chapter 14/Cautions, Page

<u>Cautions</u>

- One size does not fit all.

- Evolution, not revolution

- Comfort Zone

- Wrong tool for job

- Sincerity is critical

Chapter 15/Hard Cases, Page

<u>Hints for Hard Cases</u>

- A single flower

- A Thank You

- A small compliment

- A hug

- A pat on the hand

- A smile

- A card

Chapter 15/Hard Cases, Page

Hard Case Review

- Was my gesture simple enough?

- Was my gesture nurturing?

- Would another gesture have worked better?

- Does my friend have things that are bothering her so that the gesture is overshadowed?

- Was the occasion proper?

- Was the timing proper?

- Did I do it okay, flub it?

- Was her reaction for the gesture or for me or for something else?

Chapter 16/Sex, Page

Do List for the Romantic Side of Sex

- Do plan to take your lover away occasionally to a romantic spot.

- Do return to your honeymoon spot.

- Do understand that the orgasms experienced by men and women are very different. Women like to continue to be held and loved after the climax.

- Do express appreciation of the person, not just the body.

- Do take time. Let passion build.

- Do include a lot of holding and touching.

- Do discuss what you each enjoy.

- Do express your appreciation for spending time and sharing each other.

- Do think of other gestures on occasions of passion. For example, flowers and, of course, words.

- Do remember sex is sharing. It is not a right, obligation or duty.

- Do try to be spontaneous. Try different things, different times.

Chapter 16/Sex, Page

<u>Don't List of the Romantic Side of Sex</u>

- Don't think of your satisfaction only. This is a time for sharing like no other.

- Don't look at the union as an end, but part of a relationship.

- Don't forget to take care of your own body. Unless it is specifically a turn on for your partner, shave and bathe. Most women do not find it sexy to be sand papered by a beard or have a smell like you just spent a week doing hard labor.

- Don't turn on the TV right after love, or during.

- Don't assume that owning a penis creates an understanding of what your partner wants. Discuss what is enjoyed.

- Don't abruptly leave after you have done you thing. Linger.

- Don't do the same things all the time. This produces routine and routine can be deadly.

- Don't get stuck in "every Saturday night," unless that is really what both want.

CONCLUSION

This book has been a joy to put together. This is not to say that it has not involved work. As any author will tell you, writing a book or article is work. In this case, the work was largely offset by the joy of spending time in thinking and writing about romance.

Romantic thought, just like romantic gesturing, blesses those engaged in the activity. Writing about being romantic has taken me back over many pleasant memories. I feel enriched by the process. I am curious about whether Peg noticed any differences. It is entirely possible that she got an extra hug or whatever. On the other hand, we hug quite a bit and an extra one would seem normal.

You have noted that I brought a few personal examples involving Peg into the book. She is my focal point of romance. (See the dedication.) The personal examples came naturally because they are real and because this subject is very personal. It would be difficult to write this book if I were a non-romantic researching the subject in the library. To write of romance is a romantic gesture. It is to experience an overflowing of feeling and a wish to share it.

Why this passion to share? I guess it is because by giving, I gain. Romance is a multiplying force. By giving you some of my feelings or ideas, you are more joyful, or I hope so. But I am, also, through the act of giving. It truly becomes a win-win if your significant other is also involved.

In a very real sense, this little sharing is exactly what we need in our world today. Oh, don't get excited. I'm not suggesting that this guide is the key to world peace or anything of the kind. Well, maybe something of the kind. If a few more became more romantic than they used to be, some positive thing is occurring. Where there are positives, romantic gestures, love and kindness, then there is a bit less room for hate and violence. That's OK.

If that's true, and I firmly believe it is, then the same principle would hold if kindness were the subject just as much as with the subject being a broadening of romance. What would happen if folks were a bit kinder to others? Interesting thought, not new, but interesting. Maybe some one should write a book....

0-595-25610-4